WIN
AT
POKER

BY
JEFF RUBENS

DOVER PUBLICATIONS, INC.
NEW YORK

Published in Canada by General Publishing Company, Ltd., 30 Lesmill Road, Don Mills, Toronto, Ontario.
Published in the United Kingdom by Constable and Company, Ltd.

This Dover edition, first published in 1984, is an unabridged republication of the edition originally published by Funk & Wagnalls, New York, in 1968.

Manufactured in the United States of America
Dover Publications, Inc., 31 East 2nd Street, Mineola, N.Y. 11501

Library of Congress Cataloging in Publication Data

Rubens, Jeff.
  Win at poker.

  Reprint. Originally published: New York : Funk & Wagnalls, 1968.
  Includes index.
  1. Poker. I. Title.
[GV1251.R8 1984]   795.41'2   83-20556
ISBN 0-486-24626-4

To F.M.T. and A.H.M.

I would like to acknowledge the invaluable assistance of two people who helped make this book possible. First, a poker expert (to whom I will give the pseudonym S. Nail) who generously checked the technical portions and backed my guesses with his authority. Second, my wife, Beth, who contributed patience and grammar.

CONTENTS

INTRODUCTION

To illustrate my primary objective in this book, let me use myself as an example, by considering my position with respect to a game I know very little about. Soccer, for example. I understand the basic rules of soccer, but of strategy and tactics I know nothing. Recently, professional soccer teams have been brought to the United States and I have watched one or two games on television. I can tell, of course, when a goal is scored, but I have no clue to the *cause* of the goal. It may have been scored as the result of superior offensive play, inferior defensive play, blind luck, a foul undetected by the referee, or as the result of some stratagem I know nothing about. Still, whatever the cause, the goal will always look the same to me.

In order to appreciate the maneuvers of the soccer players, I must be able to understand the underlying reasons behind their various actions. I must have some knowledge of the techniques they employ to achieve their strategical objectives. In the absence of my own knowledge, this function must be filled by a sportscaster—he will make the game intelligible to me through his comments and descriptions. The better he is, the deeper will be my understanding, and the greater will be my enjoyment.

My intention is to be a good sportscaster in this book. If I am successful, you will be more knowledgeable with regard to poker. You will know not only who won a hand, but why.

You also will know whether the winner succeeded in winning as much as he could have.

But there is an important difference between your poker and my soccer. I have no hope of learning the techniques of soccer with the aim of personal participation. (Table tennis is more my speed.) On the other hand, you have every right to expect to be able to master poker technique *and be able to apply it yourself.* In fact, there is no reason why you should not become a winner at the poker table if you master the principles in this book.

Alas, there is more to learning than simply reading books. I could read and memorize every book ever written on soccer and still not be able to kick the ball properly. When you are learning for purposes of your own participation *there is no substitute for practice.* Thus, the most important part of your poker education is actually playing poker. Throughout this book, you will gain some "playing" experience through the example hands and brief quizzes which will enable you to apply the principles set forth in each chapter. But even this is no substitute for actually sitting at a card table with live players to analyze, a real stack of chips to manage, and actual cards—not mere printed symbols—for you to see and remember.

Here we come to the major difference between this book and other poker books (or books on any game for that matter). I will offer not only sound advice for winning—do this, don't do that, follow this principle, don't be misled by that fallacy, and so on—but also instruction on *how to profit from your poker experiences.* In short, this is really a book on how to *learn* poker. Be under no illusions that this book will make you a poker expert in ten easy lessons, or change you from a losing player to a winning player overnight. What it will do—if you contribute your careful attention and a modicum of energy—is familiarize you with the essential workings of poker, the hidden mechanisms which control winning and losing, and enable you to see them in action at the card table.

I used myself as an example a few paragraphs ago; now it's your turn. Consider yourself. You see a deal of poker played. You may be a spectator (kibitzer, in cardplayers' jargon), a participant in the game not involved in the deal, or even a player with a financial interest. You see money put into the pot. You see the player with the best hand win. (It may even, on occasion, be you.) You see the pot gathered in. *But you really do not understand why or how this happened any more than I understand why or how a soccer goal is scored.*

It is my intention to change that state of affairs. Of course, I need your cooperation to do it. In particular, I request two favors, and need I mention that you are really doing them for yourself?

1. This book is intended for two groups of people: first, those with little or no poker experience who would like to learn what the game is all about and how to play it and enjoy it; second, those who know something about poker and who cannot afford not to know more.

I am speaking now to the second group. When you read this book, make believe you know nothing of how poker is (or should be) played. True, you can read the early chapters a little faster than the uninitiated. But *do* read them and try not to be prejudiced by what you already know (or think you know). The saying about "a little knowledge" was never more appropriate than with regard to the game of poker. One or two incorrect preconceived notions can do you more harm than any three books can undo.

2. This message is for everyone. This book is not a novel designed for your enjoyment and captivation; nor is it a collection of ancedotes aimed at your amusement. It is

rather a serious study of the game of poker, and its eventual goal is your edification and profit. (I have always felt that instructional books on money games should be treated as an investment. You have invested the purchase price and the amount of time required to master the contents and should be interested in maximizing your profits.)

It should therefore be apparent that this is *not* the type of book that can be read at one sitting. If you sit down at the beginning of a rainy afternoon and say to yourself, "Today I am going to learn how to play poker," you will gain little more from this book than you would from Einstein's "Theory of Relativity" read at the same speed. In fact, you should skim over the chapters you have already read (to refresh your memory) before proceeding to new material.

Many chapters include short quizzes. Their purpose is twofold: first, to offer some experience in simulated real-life situations; second, to offer the reader the opportunity of checking his comprehension of the principles presented. Don't rush. If you find yourself floundering on a quiz, don't be ashamed to reread the chapter in question. No one is looking.

I have spent a good deal of time and energy organizing this book carefully and attempting to present all the important principles of poker in logical order. Don't sell yourself short by racing through to a section that particularly appeals to you or by failing to give each chapter your full attention.

Proceed at your own pace and you will be learning under the best possible conditions. And that, perhaps, is the most important single piece of advice I can give on the learning of the game of poker.

Finally, a word about the scope of the material. At the beginning, I will assume the reader has never played poker. Accordingly, the first few chapters are devoted to fundamentals. From then on, however, each section encompasses several levels of poker sophistication. For each poker form, I start with essentials and range all the way up to advanced strategy and expert tactics.

The quizzes and examples show similar diversity. Some are elementary, designed to insure adequate basic knowledge. Some are intermediate, intended to provide practical experience and realistic illustrations of the poker situations one may reasonably expect to encounter. A few are more advanced, aimed at showing the type of thinking done by advanced players and exposing you to the fascination of poker analysis. Thus, if you are a typical reader, you will find some quiz questions easy, some "about your speed," and some beyond your knowledge. This is as it should be, and you will be able to gauge your progress by how far into each quiz your understanding extends. Because of their nature, the quizzes form part of the text—new principles and advanced tactics are introduced—and should be so considered. The examination format is the most convenient way to sit you down in a poker situation and have you think for yourself to see whether you can apply what you have learned.

O N E

◎ ◎ ◎ ◎ ◎

The Rules of Poker

Along with the majority of popular card games, poker is played with a standard deck of 52 cards. The four suits (spades, hearts, diamonds, and clubs) are equals—one is as good as another—but the cards within each suit have an order of rank which is of great importance. The order is the usual one: ace (A) is highest, followed by king (K), queen (Q), jack (J), 10, 9, 8, 7, 6, 5, 4, 3, and 2 (or deuce), which is lowest.

There are literally thousands of different forms of poker, but they all adhere to one basic idea: poker is every man for himself, and each player attempts to make the best-valued poker hand. Bets are placed as to which player has the best hand (just as bets are placed on which horse will win a race) and that player wins all the bets (usually called the pot).

A poker hand consists of five cards. The hands are ranked in accordance with their relative frequencies. The rarer the hand (and thus the more difficult to get), the higher its value as a poker hand. Since the rank of poker hands plays an essential part in determining the outcome of each deal of poker, it is necessary to memorize the relative values of all poker hands.

The Rules of Poker

The highest-ranking poker hand (when there are no **wild cards**—a term I will explain later—in the game) is the **straight flush.** Only one out of every 65,000 poker hands falls into this category! A straight flush consists of five cards *in the same suit* and *in sequence*. For example,

♠ 10   ♠ 9   ♠ 8   ♠ 7   ♠ 6
and
♦ A   ♦ K   ♦ Q   ♦ J   ♦ 10

are straight flushes, whereas

♠ 10   ♠ 9   ♣ 8   ♠ 7   ♠ 6   (not all the same suit)
and
♦ A   ♦ K   ♦ Q   ♦ J   ♦ 9   (not in sequence)

are not. Among straight flushes, the one containing the highest-ranking card is superior. Thus, the second example hand above is higher ranking than the first. In the spade hand, the top card is a 10, whereas the diamond hand contains an ace. A straight flush headed by an ace (the highest-ranking poker hand of all) is usually dignified with the name **royal flush.** Only one in 650,000 poker hands is a royal flush. (So don't expect one too often!)

The next best hand is **four of a kind.** This is a hand with four cards of the same rank, such as

♠ A   ♥ A   ♦ A   ♣ A   ♥ 2   (four aces)
or
♠ 3   ♥ 3   ♦ 3   ♣ 3   ♦ J   (four threes)

9

The nature of the fifth card is irrelevant. Between such hands, the one with four of the higher rank is superior. Thus, four aces outranks four kings, which in turn is higher than four queens and so on.

Next in line is a **full house**: three cards of one rank and two of another rank. Full houses are designated by the rank of the three of a kind, and the higher this rank, the higher the full house. The following hands are given in order of rank:

♠ A	♥ A	♦ A	♥ 2	♣ 2	(aces full)
♥ K	♦ K	♣ K	♠ 9	♥ 9	(kings full)
♠ 9	♥ 9	♣ 9	♦ Q	♣ Q	(nines full)
♠ 2	♦ 2	♣ 2	♥ A	♣ A	(deuces full)

Notice that the rank of the three of a kind determines the value of the full house.

After a full house comes a **flush**: all five cards in the same suit (such as five spades or five clubs). The straight flush—discussed above—is a very special kind of flush. Between flushes, the one with the higher card is higher ranking. If the top cards are equal, the one with the higher ranking *second* card takes precedence. The following flushes are listed in order of rank:

♠ A	♠ J	♠ 9	♠ 7	♠ 4	(ace-high flush)
♠ K	♠ Q	♠ 10	♠ 9	♠ 6	(king-high flush)
♠ Q	♠ J	♠ 6	♠ 5	♠ 4	(queen-jack flush)
♠ Q	♠ 10	♠ 9	♠ 8	♠ 6	(queen-ten flush)

A **straight**, the next hand, consists of five cards in sequence (e.g.: A-K-Q-J-10, 9-8-7-6-5), regardless of suit. If all the cards happen to be of the same suit, we have our old friend the straight flush (which, as you now can see, is a hand that is *both* a straight and a flush). Between straights, the one with the higher top card is the higher ranking. Thus, A-K-Q-J-10 is the highest-ranking straight, K-Q-J-10-9 is next, and so forth.

In modern poker, the ace is usually considered the lowest card as well as the highest when it comes to forming straights. The lowest straight is therefore 5-4-3-2-A. (You cannot, however, "turn the corner." Thus holding 3-2-A-K-Q is not a straight; in fact, it is nothing at all.) The five-high straight (5-4-3-2-A) is sometimes called a **bicycle** or a **wheel**.

Next in line is **three of a kind** (sometimes called **triplets**): three of the five cards in the hand are of the same rank. The other two are unmatched. Again suits are irrelevant and the higher the rank of the three similar cards, the higher the hand. Thus, A-A-A-3-2 (three aces) is higher ranking than K-K-K-Q-J (three kings).

Two pairs is next and the title describes the hand well: two sets of two cards of the same rank. Between hands with two pairs, the one with the higher pair is the higher ranking. (If the high pairs are of the same rank, the rank of the low pairs determines the rank of the hands.) If, through incredible coincidence, there are two hands in which both pairs are of identical ranks, the rank of the extra card determines which hand ranks higher. The following hands with two pairs are listed in order of rank:

♠ A	♥ A	♠ 6	♦ 6	♣ 7	(aces up or aces over sixes)
♠ K	♥ K	♥ 5	♦ 5	♥ Q	(kings up or kings over fives)
♠ K	♥ K	♥ 3	♦ 3	♠ 7	(kings over threes)
♠ Q	♥ Q	♠ J	♣ J	♥ K	(queens over jacks, king next)
♦ Q	♣ Q	♥ J	♦ J	♣ 7	(queens over jacks, seven next)

If you can't get two pairs, the next best thing you can do is get **one pair**. Between hands with one pair, the higher pair determines the higher hand. (If the pairs are the same, then the higher-ranking odd card determines the rank; if these cards are equal, the next higher odd card, etc.) The following hands are listed in order of rank:

♠ A	♥ A	♦ 7	♥ 6	♣ 4	(pair of aces)
♠ Q	♥ Q	♦ 9	♥ 8	♣ 2	(pair of queens, nine next)
♦ Q	♣ Q	♥ 7	♦ 6	♣ 3	(pair of queens, seven next)
♠ 2	♥ 2	♠ A	♥ K	♣ Q	(pair of deuces)

Last and least are hands with **no pair** (and nothing else of value such as a straight or flush). These hands are disgustingly common (about half of all poker hands have no pair). Between hands with no pair, the one with the higher odd card ranks higher; in case of ties, the one with the second-higher odd card, and so forth. Thus, A-7-5-4-3 (ace high) is ranked above K-Q-J-9-5 (king high, queen next) which is higher than K-10-8-6-4 (king high, ten next).

Here is a summary of the ranks of poker hands (highest first):

Straight flush	All in suit, ranks in sequence
Four of a kind	Four of the same rank
Full house	Three of one rank, two of another
Flush	All in the same suit
Straight	Ranks of cards in sequence
Three of a kind	Three cards of one rank
Two pairs	Two cards of one rank, two of another
One pair	Two cards of one rank, three unmatched
No pair	Five unmatched cards

The Rules of Poker

If you have never played poker, or if you cannot repeat this table from memory, forward and backward, take a deck of cards and deal out hands of five cards for each of a group of imaginary players. Examine each hand and determine its category by referring to the above chart. (This exercise will give you an idea of how hard it is to get one of the higher-ranking hands.)

After you have done this for a while, take a group of hands and make as few changes as necessary to get each hand into one of the higher categories.

THE BETTING

The ranks of the various hands determine which player wins and which players lose in a deal of poker. *How much they win, or lose, is determined by the betting.* It is the betting phase which determines the winners and losers in poker, for in the long run everyone gets his fair share of good cards.

In each deal of poker there will be one or more **betting rounds** in which each of the players has the opportunity to wager that he will have the best poker hand at the conclusion of the deal. Within each betting round, the bets must be equalized. For instance, if Player A has bet one dollar, and Player B wishes to bet against him (i.e., Player B thinks his hand is as good or better than that of Player A), then B must also bet one dollar. All bets, which are usually made by means of chips, are placed in the pot in the center of the table. If a player does not wish to enter the betting at any stage, he may relinquish his chance to win the pot by discarding his hand face down. A player who does so is said to have **dropped** from the pot. He need put no more money into the pot, but he has no chance to win, even if it later develops that his was the superior poker hand.

After the bets have been equalized in the final betting round, there is a showdown. All players who are still **in the pot** (i.e., have bet as much as anyone else) expose their cards and the player with the best hand wins the pot.

There are two questions that arise frequently regarding the showdown. Let's avoid later uncertainty by dealing with them at once.

First, there is the matter of obligation to show a hand in the showdown. Suppose the following situation arises: Al and Bob are the only two players in the showdown. After the final betting round, Al announces three jacks and shows his cards to substantiate his claim. Bob, perhaps disgustedly (he may have three tens himself or some hand he is ashamed to show), throws his cards down and refuses to let anyone look at them.

Question: Is Bob under any obligation to show his cards?
Answer: Yes.

In a showdown, all hands should be shown. It is not a violation of the rules not to show your cards if not asked to do so, but any player has the right to request that they be exposed. (We will see later that information gained from these situations may prove very valuable when it comes to learning the style and analyzing the level of skill of your opponent.)

Do not confuse the case above with the following: Charlie and Dick remain in a pot and Charlie makes a bet which Dick does not wish to call. Dick therefore drops and throws away his cards; Charlie wins the pot. Neither Charlie nor Dick is obligated to show his cards to any other player. It is only when the outcome of a deal is determined by a showdown (that is, when two or more players have bet equally) that all the hands must be shown.

The second issue is the misreading of the cards.

Question: If a player overlooks a winning hand, and miscalls his values, is he entitled to the pot? May or should someone else point out an error of this kind?

Answer: There is a poker saying covering this situation, "The cards speak for themselves."

It is not necessary to call a hand correctly in order to gain the rights to the pot stemming from the value of the cards. Furthermore, any player may (and should) call attention to such an error. (Spectators, however, should refrain from making gratuitous remarks.) Such corrections are not necessarily valid after the cards have been mixed, although most poker groups attempt to settle such matters amicably rather than stick to the precise letter of the law.

Getting back to the betting itself, there are three actions a player may take *at his turn*. (Turns within a betting round proceed clockwise around the table.) These actions are: **check, bet,** and **drop.** A check is a noncommittal move—it announces the lack of desire of the player to bet at this time, but it does not forfeit his rights to the pot. Of course, a player may not check if another player has made a bet during the current betting round. Once a bet is made, everyone must "put up or shut up," that is, match the bet or drop from the pot.

A drop occurs when a player decides he does not wish to bet on his hand as the best poker hand. If some other player has made a bet and you do not wish to match it, you drop out of the pot by turning your cards face down on the table. This relieves you of the obligation to spend any more money but, of course, you also relinquish your chance to win the pot.

A bet is an expression of opinion that the bettor has, or eventually will have, the best poker hand. There are three types of bets: the **initial bet** on a betting round, made before any other player has bet, which issues a challenge to the other participants to match the bet or drop from the pot; the **call**, in which a player stays in the pot by matching the amount previously bet; the **raise,** a bet of *more* than the amount previously bet, which forces the other players to match an even higher amount if they wish to remain in the deal and retain a chance to win the pot.

Within a betting round, each player is given the opportunity to make a bet or, if the circumstances permit, to check, call, raise, or drop. The turn to bet passes clockwise (to the left), the player with the right to bet first being designated by the rules of the form of poker being played. The turn to bet continues around the table until each player has matched the amount bet by all the others or has dropped out of the pot. (On infrequent occasions, no player will wish to bet; thus, each will check when it comes his turn. When this occurs, the betting round is said to be "checked out." The game proceeds as if a normal betting round had been completed. In certain forms of poker, a check-out on the first betting round necessitates a new deal.)

Here are two examples of complete betting rounds involving four players: Al, Bob, Charlie, and Dick.

Example One: Al, who is designated to act first, checks; Bob bets (let us say $1); Charlie drops; Dick calls; Al calls. The bets have now been equalized, so the betting round is over. It may be convenient to examine this in tabular form.

AL	BOB	CHARLIE	DICK		BOB	
* Check	Bet($1)	Drop	Call($1)	AL	◯	CHARLIE
Call($1.)	—	—	—		DICK	

* Designated as first to act.

Notice that Al was permitted to check because no player had yet made a bet. This privilege did not extend to Charlie, because he was forced to match Bob's bet or drop from the pot. When the turn to bet had passed completely around the table, it returned to Al because the bets were not yet equalized. At the end of the round, each player who was still active (i.e., had not dropped) had bet $1.

Example Two: Al bets ($1); Bob drops; Charlie raises, betting $2—$1 to call Al's bet, $1 to raise him; Dick calls for $2 as he must match the total amount bet by Charlie; Al calls the raise, but he need put in only $1 since he already has $1 in the pot.

AL	BOB	CHARLIE	DICK			
* Bet($1)	Drop	Raise($2)	Call($2)	AL	◯	CHARLIE
Call($1)	—	—	—		DICK	

Designated as first to act.

Each player who is still active has bet $2 on this betting round, so the bets are equalized and the round is over.

There are various rules which may be applied to limit the size of bets. For the present, we will assume that the **limit betting** rule is in effect. That is, there is a fixed limit (be it a penny, a quarter, a dollar, or whatever) on the amount a player may bet at any one time. Other betting methods will be discussed in Chapter Eleven. The inexperienced player should, however, restrict himself to games in which there is limit betting.

Games with limit betting sometimes have a further restriction on the number of raises allowed within a betting round. The most popular rule (which meets with my approval as the best of its type) is that there may be no more than three raises in any one betting round. The limit on the number of raises (if any) is one of the many "table rules" that must be agreed on before a poker game begins.

WIN AT POKER

In most poker games, betting is accomplished through the use of chips. At the beginning of the game, each player purchases a stack of chips from a banker (who also redeems the chips at the conclusion of play).

THE ANTE

Now that we know the two fundamentals of poker—the value of the hands and the mechanics of betting—we are ready to examine the mechanics of a complete deal.

Each poker deal begins with the payment of an amount (called the **ante**) to the pot by each player. This amount is usually small compared with the size of an allowable bet.

The ante represents each player's **overhead**—his payment for the right to obtain cards and have a chance to win the pot. The purpose of the ante is twofold. First, it starts the pot off with a fixed amount that gives the players something to aim at when they make their bets. If for no other reason, a player may make a bet in the hope of winning the antes which are already in the pot. Second, the existence of the ante adds action and excitement to the game. Without the ante, it would be a possible strategy not to play any hand unless it was extremely good. After all, it would cost nothing to sit back and wait for a virtual sure thing. This method of play will result in losses when there is an ante. Whether or not you choose to play, there will always be an ante payment on each deal. Those few times you bet (and win) will not compensate for your many small losses. Thus, the ante provides an incentive to bet on less than a certainty, and stimulates the betting. We will see later that the relative size of the ante and the initial bet plays a large part in determining winning poker strategy.

18

The Rules of Poker

Here is a tip which will not win you any money, but which can help make any poker game you play in more pleasant. All poker games have at least one argument per session over which player did not put his ante into the pot. It goes something like this: there are eight players and the ante for each deal is a quarter; each pot therefore starts with two dollars. After the cards have been dealt, someone (let's say Al) notices there is only $1.75 in the center of the table; Bob, Charlie and Dick all swear virtuously that they have contributed their quarters; Ed mutters, "Here we go again" under his breath; Frank accuses George of not "anteing up"; George tells Frank he knows his quarter is in because he took change while handing Charlie his beer; Dick points out that it is probably Harry, who hasn't put in his ante several times already; Harry rises from his chair . . . etc. Result: loss of time, loss of energy, general hard feeling.

The solution to this problem is absurdly simple: have each dealer pay up the entire ante. The deal passes clockwise after each hand. Thus, after the deal has gone completely around the table, each player will have paid his fair share of antes. And all the problems revolving around who threw in a chip and who didn't (which nobody remembers anyway) will disappear.

POKER ETHICS

Poker is unusual (almost unique) in that standards of conduct are as important as technical laws. Accordingly, we will treat the subject of poker ethics on an equal footing with poker laws.

WIN AT POKER

Although the basic laws of poker are universally established, acceptable standards of conduct vary wildly from one game to the next. Poker is played by widely differing groups, from the hardboiled serious players in a club or private game to the ladies at a social gathering. Unlike bridge, and other games in which standards of ethical behavior are written into the rules of the game, the ethics of a poker game are determined by the players-of-the-moment. What may be acceptable behavior in one game may be scandalous in another. A good example is **coffeehousing,** making unnecessary remarks or gestures (such as saying, "I have a flush and I dare you to call my bet," whether or not you really have a flush). In a rough-and-tumble club atmosphere, or in a serious game, such tactics will be widely disregarded. The boys in a college dorm might think this ploy tricky and might or might now allow such remarks to be made. The ladies' afternoon social will almost certainly brand a coffeehouser as a sharp player—the next thing to a cheat—and the use of such tactics may make her a social pariah.

Except that superserious players (especially self-styled experts) usually play "anything goes," there is little relationship between the outlook on poker ethics and the skill of the players. It is really a question of the personalities of the players. If you think I'm wrong, why don't *you* try to come out a winner in a "social" ladies' afternoon game—it's not that easy.

Since you want to be a socially acceptable poker player (you can't win money from people who don't let you into their game), it follows that you must conform to whatever the prevailing ethical standards are where you play. If you don't happen to know what they are, simply ask one of the regular players. Needless to say, if you are a regular player yourself, you may wish to attempt to influence the standards of behavior adopted by your own group. By all means do so if it is important to you, especially if it affects your enjoyment of the game. But if it doesn't matter very much to you—and it doesn't to most people—I recommend giving in to the opposing point of view if it is expressed. Everyone appreciates someone who concedes a point every now and then; and the more you are liked the less people will notice how much you are winning.

While checking on the ethical standards of a poker game you are about to play in there is one issue which you must be absolutely clear about: **sandbagging.** Venturing a guess as to the origin of the term, I would say it probably stems from the days when poker was associated with riverboat gamblers fleecing the patrons traveling on steamboats on the Mississippi River. In those days, when you wanted to do someone in, you sneaked up behind him and bopped him one with a (presumably well-filled) sandbag. In poker, to sandbag is to check and then raise a bet made by another player. When you sandbag, you are laying a trap, hoping that another player will bet; you now make a higher bet, making it more expensive for the other player(s) to stay in the pot. (If you yourself had made a bet, the other player(s) could stay in for the size of an ordinary bet rather than a raised bet.) Usually, you sandbag with either a very good hand— hoping to win a large pot—or, on rare occasions, as a bluff (in which you make believe you have a strong hand, hoping the other players will drop out of the pot).

No serious player, or serious poker game, can have any logical objection to the tactic of sandbagging; it is, in fact, one of the things that livens up the game of poker. On the other hand, however, there are certain players who feel offended by this strategy. Nobody knows why, and probably nobody will find out until some clever psychology student decides to write his doctoral thesis on "The Betting Habits of American Poker Players."

In any event, sandbagging in the wrong poker game seems to be about as serious a crime as one can commit against poker society and its unwritten variable ethical code. Hence my advice: make certain you understand the policy of a poker game on sandbagging before you sit down to play.

POKER LAWS

It is understandable that poker, being a game of individuals and personalities, should accept the burden of having each individual group determine its own ethical standards. However, it is remarkable (and, in fact, a shame) that poker players have never accepted a uniform code of laws. I do not mean laws regarding the normal procedures of the game (everyone agrees on the relative rank of the hands, the mechanics of the betting, and so on) but rather the methods of adjudicating irregularities: misdeals, exposed cards, improper amounts put into the pot, etc.

The pitiful lack of universality of poker laws dealing with irregularities has led to the paradoxical situation in which one cannot sit down to play a game of poker without determining the rules under which the game will be conducted. (The special rules adopted by a poker game are usually called the **house rules**.) So, in addition to determining the ethical standards of a poker group, one must also determine which set of laws (or what conglomeration of individual laws) controls the game.

The Rules of Poker

No doubt you agree with me that this is a silly state of affairs. The danger of arguments on some undiscussed point ("But we didn't specify paragraph 53 subsection 4c, so lines 7 through 9 must apply and *I* win the pot.") is great, and it is a terrible burden on the players to have to remember which rules are in force. Furthermore, there is always someone upon whose shoulders falls the burden of settling disputes. King Solomon was an amateur if he never attempted to untangle a poker quarrel.

It is easy to point an accusing finger at the cause of the present difficulty. Poker is a very old game. Some authorities say its origins go back as far as the invention of playing cards! As the game evolved into present-day poker, the rules evolved as well, each generation of poker players experimenting with and modifying the rules. Eventually, certain poker traditions dealing with the crucial area of irregularities sprang up and became entrenched in the minds of all players. But tradition is a hard thing to shake off, and when the game advanced into modern times, the classic rules for dealing with nonstandard situations were carried along, whether or not they applied to the modern forms of poker and, if they did apply, *whether or not they were sensible.*

At some time during the twentieth century, the popularity of poker grew enormously (and has been rising ever since). Far more players than ever before took up the game seriously and many of them took long and intelligent looks at the traditional rules—and detected flaws. Quite logically, they instituted changes in their own games, designed to make the game fairer, more interesting, and more enjoyable. Regrettably, every poker group resolved these difficulties in a slightly different way. Thus, not only was there no uniform poker code, but when it came time for the "rules" of poker to be published in authoritative manuals, what choice was there but to print the traditional rules—the only set of rules in complete use by more than one or two individual poker groups?

Thus, despite apparently logical action on all sides, poker has never straightened out its laws. Because of this, confusion and occasional inequity have been heaped upon generations of poker players. It is a tribute to the fascination of the game that it has been able to survive this terrible handicap.

It is quite possible that the attempt I am now about to make to straighten out the laws of poker will be futile; it may even make things worse. But liking poker as much as I do (as I hope you will also when you have finished this book) I feel it would be a dereliction of duty not to make the attempt. In the appendix I present what I call "The Modern Laws of Poker." I compare modern trends to traditional laws and point out deficiencies in the old laws and how they can be remedied. I hasten to add that these laws do not represent merely my personal opinion of how poker should be played. Rather, they are a distillation of the thinking of the leading poker experts and lawmakers over a considerable period of time.

Needless to say, I strongly recommend that you adopt this code for your own poker game. But more than that, I hope that you will suggest the use of the modern laws in whatever poker game you find yourself.

Whatever the effects of the development of poker, its history is a fascinating one. Although we cannot be certain of its early evolution, poker historians are in almost universal agreement on many facts.

Poker is believed to be derived from one of the earliest card games played in Persia and China. An early Persian game, *as nas*, is quite similar to modern-day poker in principle, for the players bet on who will have the highest-ranking combination of cards. In this game, the entire deck is dealt out, five cards to each player, and the size of the pack varies with the number of participants.

Variations of poker appeared in Europe in the seventeenth and eighteenth centuries. The name of the American game presumably comes from the French name *poque,* and the game became American after the Louisiana Purchase. It is now a worldwide game. If there were any out-of-the-way places where poker had not spread, they were infected by American servicemen, especially during World War II.

Although poker is played everywhere, it is generally regarded as an American game, even though its roots are anything but American.

QUIZ

I have included a bit of poker history because I felt you were entitled to "know the score" on the conditions under which the game is played. (Don't let my electioneering through exaggeration distract you from your pursuit of poker.)

My soapboxing about the laws was deliberately placed in this chapter so that I could distract you before presenting the first quiz. No fair peeking at the first part of the chapter when you try it.

In this quiz I present ten poker hands. Your task is as follows:

First, classify each hand by its poker name.

Second, list the hands (just writing the identifying letters of the hands is easiest) *in order of poker rank;* highest ranking first, then next highest ranking, etc.

Third, imagine for the moment that you were given the right to attempt to improve each of these hands by discarding any of the cards you wished and drawing an equal number of fresh cards from the deck. Make a guess at which cards you should throw away to give you the best chance of improving the hand to a higher category. (This may seem a purposeless exercise at present, but it's really extremely important as you will see in the next chapter.)

Here are the ten hands:

A.	♠ 6	♥ 3	♦ 3	♣ 7	♣ 3
B.	♦ 10	♠ 6	♠ Q	♦ 2	♦ 7
C.	♥ 3	♥ Q	♥ J	♠ 5	♣ J
D.	♠ K	♦ J	♦ 10	♥ 9	♣ K
E.	♦ 2	♦ K	♦ Q	♦ J	♦ 5
F.	♠ J	♣ J	♦ 9	♦ 8	♦ 7
G.	♥ 5	♣ 8	♠ 7	♠ 9	♠ 6
H.	♦ 4	♥ 9	♠ 8	♣ 7	♠ 6
I.	♠ 8	♦ 9	♥ 9	♣ 8	♠ 9
J.	♠ 8	♦ 9	♥ 10	♣ 8	♠ 9

SOLUTIONS

Here are the hands in order of poker rank:

1. I (Full house) "Nines full" or "Nines full eights"
Three cards of one rank and two of another. The higher ranking hands (straight flush and four of a kind) were omitted to emphasize their relative infrequency.

2. E (Flush) "King-high flush"
All five cards of the same suit.

3. G (Straight) "Nine-high straight"
Five cards in sequence.

4. A (Three of a kind) "Three threes," or (colloquially) "Trip threes" (a nickname for "triplet threes")

5. J (Two pairs) "Nines over eights" or "Nines up"
Two cards in each of two different ranks

6. D (One pair) "Pair of kings"
Two cards of the same rank.

7. C (One pair) "Pair of jacks, queen next"
Notice that the pair of kings outranks the pair of jacks because of the superior rank of the pair.

8. F (One pair) "Pair of jacks, nine next"
This hand is inferior to the other pair of jacks because of the inferior rank of the supporting card.

9. B (No pair) "Queen high"

10. H (No pair) "Nine high"
Among the hands with no pair, the one with the highest card ranks highest. So Hand B (with a queen high) outranks Hand H (with a nine high).

The process of discarding useless cards and taking new ones is called **drawing** because you draw fresh cards from the pack. Let's consider the hands in order of rank and examine the best method of drawing cards in each case.

To hands I (full house), E (flush), and G (straight), no cards at all should be drawn. All five cards are needed to make up the hand and the discard of any card would break up a hand which is already of high value.

To hand A (three of a kind), two cards should be drawn, the two odd cards (♠ 6, ♣ 7) being discarded. This gives us two chances to draw the fourth three (which would be a superb hand) and retains the chance of making a full house by picking up two new cards of the same rank.

To hand J (two pairs), one card should be drawn, the unmatched card (♥ 10) being thrown away. We hope to pick up an eight or a nine, giving us a full house.

To hands D, C, and F (one pair), three cards should be drawn, the three unmatched cards being discarded in each case. The main hope is to turn the pair into three of a kind and there is also a chance of picking up a new pair and turning the hand into two pairs.

Hands B and H (no pair) are so inferior that the best thing to do is to throw away all five cards and try five new ones. (Some poker groups restrict the maximum draw to three cards, however.)

Note that it is usually wrong to throw away sure values in the hope of hitting a long shot and making a very good hand. It is tempting, for example, to throw away one of the kings from Hand D in an attempt to draw a queen and thereby make a straight. This is exactly the kind of temptation that you must avoid if you are to become a winning poker player.

The form of poker in which the technique of drawing is used is called, sensibly, **draw poker**. Draw poker is one of the two major forms of poker and will be discussed in detail in the next chapter. One of the fascinations of this form of poker is that it is sometimes correct to deviate from the theoretically correct draws (illustrated in the above examples). We will discuss these exceptions in due course but we will first learn to walk before we try to run.

YOUR POKER RATING

How well did you score in the quiz? If you missed anywhere in the ranking of the hands, or even if there was any uncertainty in your mind at any point, go back and review the relative values of the poker hands.

If you were able to pass the hand-ranking part of this test, you know more about poker than at least 50 percent of the people who play it! This statement may seem amazing but it is quite conservative when placed next to other estimates; some authorities believe that as many as 75 percent of all poker players do not know the relative values of the hands.

So here you are, already an above-average poker player without knowing the details of a single form of poker. It must be time to learn one.

T W O

◎ ◎ ◎ ◎ ◎

Draw Poker

Poker, in the form we know it today, developed in the United States in the middle of the nineteenth century. Its original form was marvelously simple: each player was dealt five cards, there was a betting round, then there was a showdown. This form of the game had the drawback that good hands were infrequent. (Consider that 12 out of 13 poker hands are no better than one pair.) Thus, there was little betting, and the gambling instinct of the participants remained largely unfulfilled.

In order to provide more incentive to stay in the pot, the draw was introduced. The resulting game, draw poker, adds this additional feature: after the betting round following the deal has been completed, each player who remains in the hand (in clockwise rotation usually starting at the dealer's left) has the opportunity to exchange a number of his original cards for new cards. (Sometimes the maximum permissible draw is three cards.) This additional phase (called the draw) adds, of course, the opportunity for an additional betting round. Thus, draw poker consists of the deal (five cards to each player), the first round of betting, the draw, the second round of betting, and the showdown.

It is easy to see why this game was considered vastly

superior to the original form of "straight" poker. The additional betting round provided more opportunity for "action." The draw added a skill factor—determining how many, and which, cards to exchange—to help overcome the luck of the deal. More good hands resulted in the showdown. Perhaps most important, there were more hands on which a player was tempted to bet.

Consider this collection:

♠8   ♠7   ♠6   ♠5   ♥2

At straight poker, this is one of the worst possible hands—only an eight high! But at draw poker, the hand offers exciting possibilities. The deuce of hearts can be exchanged for a new card. If that new card is a spade, this bad hand has become a flush; if the new card is a nine or a four, it has become a straight; and if, through really good luck, the nine or four of spades comes in the draw, someone is the proud possessor of a straight flush.

There have been hundreds of innovations in poker since the introduction of the draw, but none has had such a profound effect on the game. Not only has the original form of draw poker remained one of the most popular poker games to this day, but the draw principle—a chance to exchange cards—has been applied in many different ways to create a host of interesting newer forms of poker.

THE LAWS OF DRAW POKER

Let's put some flesh on our skeleton outline by filling in the details of the laws governing play.

WIN AT POKER

(1) The ante.

Before or during the deal, the antes are placed in the center of the table to start the pot. This is accomplished by having each player pay an ante or by having the dealer pay one ante "for the table."

(2) The deal.

As in all forms of poker, play begins with the pack being shuffled and cut. Most poker games employ two packs so that one pack can be shuffled (by an inactive player) while the other is in use.

The dealer dispenses the cards, one at a time, face down, clockwise around the table, beginning with the player on his left. The deal ends when each player has received five cards.

(3) The first betting round.

The action in the first betting round always begins with the player to the dealer's left. (This player is called the **eldest hand** or the **age**.) Betting activity proceeds in a clockwise direction, each player in turn having the opportunity to check, bet, raise, or drop.

When the bets have been equalized, that is, when every player has either dropped out of the pot or bet an amount equal to that bet by the other active players, the betting round is completed.

(4) The draw.

Along with the first betting round, the draw begins on the dealer's left. Each active player in turn, clockwise, beginning at the dealer's left, is given the opportunity to exchange one or more of his original cards for new cards from the pack. The original dealer distributes the new cards.

Draw Poker

Several points involving the draw should be noted carefully so that arguments can be avoided. First of all, the number of cards drawn by each player is public information, just as (for example) the amount of money in the pot. A player is entitled to ask, at any time, how many cards were drawn by any player. Anyone who remembers the numbers of drawn cards is obligated to divulge this information, and it is unethical to give deliberately an incorrect review of the draws. (In particular, each player is responsible for remembering the number of cards that he himself drew.)

Second, extreme care should be taken to keep the undealt portion of the pack separate from the discards. Subject to the condition that *the bottom card of the pack is never dealt,* all draws should be fulfilled from the undealt portion of the original pack when possible. The reason for the stipulation about the bottom card is this: no matter how careful the dealer is, there is always a possibility that during the process of dealing out the cards and fulfilling the draws of the active players, the bottom card of the pack may become exposed to one or more players giving them an unfair advantage. As a precaution, there is a rule that one never deals the bottom card. Some groups avoid this problem by placing a card from a different color deck face down on the bottom.

Finally, there is the problem of procedure when the pack runs out. On occasion, there will be so many active players in a deal that the original pack will not satisfy all the drawing requirements. When this occurs, the pack should be dealt out as far as possible. To obtain a new pack for use in completing the draw, combine the last card of the previous pack with all discards made *prior* to those of the player whose turn it is to draw. (Note that the discards of the players who have not yet drawn are *not* included in the new pack. A player should never have to risk receiving his own discards as part of his draw.)

The new pack, whatever its size, is shuffled and cut in the usual manner and is used to complete the draw.

(5) The second betting round.

When the draw has been completed it is time for the second betting round. Although the deal, the first betting round, and the draw all began to the left of the dealer, the second betting round begins with *the player who first bet in the first betting round*. This player is called the **opener**. (Should the opener no longer be an active player, the second betting round begins with the first active player to the left of the opener.)

With this exception, the second betting round proceeds in the same manner as the first betting round. (In most games, the limit on bets and raises is higher during the second betting round than during the first betting round.)

(6) The showdown.

After the bets have been equalized on the second betting round, all active players expose their hands in a showdown. The active player with the highest-ranking poker hand wins the entire pot. (In the rare event that two or more players have identically ranked hands, the pot is divided among the tied players.)

Remember that all the active players in the showdown must expose their cards if required to do so by any of the other players, active or not.

A SAMPLE DEAL OF DRAW POKER

Let's have a real-life illustration of the mechanics of draw poker, just to make sure there is no confusion over the rules. We will require occasional illustrative deals throughout this book so let's make further use of the poker group which was busily arguing in the previous chapter.

Our game has eight players (Al, Bob, Charlie, Dick, Ed, Frank, George, and Harry). The ante is twenty-five cents per player. Having been in a violent argument over antes a few pages ago, the group has decided to have each dealer ante $2 for the table. The betting (and raising) limit before the draw (the first betting round) is $1; the limit after the draw (the second betting round) is $2.

How typical is this game? Well, the ratio of the ante to the bet limits is fairly standard. The sum of the antes is usually about twice the bet limit before the draw, and the bet limit after the draw is usually double the limit before the draw. The actual size of the antes, and bets, however, varies from game to game. One can find games in which the ante is a penny (or even less) and games in which the ante is $25 rather than the twenty-five cents that our fictitious group uses.

As to the number of players, seven or eight is normal. The traditional number of players is eight. Are poker tables built eight-sided because eight usually play or is eight a common number of players because poker tables are built eight-sided? I don't know the answer to that one, but I *can* state that poker is workable and enjoyable regardless of the number of players. My guess is that, although individual preferences vary, poker is found more interesting with seven or eight players than with, say, only five. On the other hand, with more than seven or eight people at a card table, things tend to get cumbersome.

Our eightsome is ready for its sample deal. Harry is the dealer, with Al (to Harry's left) the eldest hand in this setup:

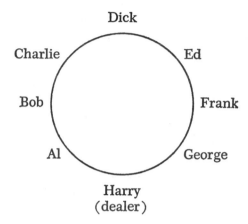

Dick

Charlie   Ed

Bob   Frank

Al   George

Harry
(dealer)

Harry passes the shuffled pack to George, who cuts. While this is being accomplished, Harry puts $2 into the center—the ante. George having cut the cards, Harry deals out five rounds of cards, face down. Here are the hands Harry deals:

Al	♥ J	♠ 7	♥ 6	♣ 5	♠ 4
Bob	♥ Q	♦ 10	♥ 9	♥ 5	♣ 2
Charlie	♦ K	♦ 4	♣ 4	♠ 3	♥ 2
Dick	♦ Q	♣ Q	♥ 7	♦ 6	♠ 2
Ed	♥ A	♥ K	♠ 5	♦ 3	♠ 3
Frank	♥ Q	♣ J	♠ 9	♣ 8	♠ 6
George	♠ A	♣ K	♠ K	♣ 9	♣ 7
Harry	♦ A	♦ J	♣ 10	♥ 10	♣ 6

If poker is new to you, actually select the cards of the sample deals from a deck and follow the action physically.

The deal has been completed. We are ready for the first betting round. Al, to the left of the dealer, is the eldest hand. Al checks. Al does not wish to bet, but he need not drop out of the pot, for no other player has yet made a bet.

Draw Poker

It is possible that no one will want to bet, in which case there will be a new deal.

Bob, with a terrible hand, also checks. Charlie has a pair of fours, but a low pair isn't worth much, especially with so many players in the game, so Charlie checks also. Dick has a pair of queens, a moderately good hand, and decides to open the pot. The bet limit is $1, so Dick puts $1 into the pot and announces his bet.

Ed, with a pair of threes, doesn't want to put in $1, so he drops. Notice that Ed can no longer check, for another player has made a bet. Having dropped from the pot, Ed discards his entire hand, face down, into the center of the table—being careful, of course, not to confuse his discards with the undealt portion of the original pack.

Frank has nothing much. His only chance for a good hand would be to discard the six and hope to draw a ten (to make a straight), but this is a very slim chance, so Frank drops.

George, with a pair of kings, has a fair hand, so he calls Dick's bet of $1 by putting $1 of his own into the pot. If George knew that Dick had only a pair of queens, he would raise the bet, putting in $2 instead of $1. (The betting limit is $1, so George is allowed to match Dick's bet and bet an additional $1.) The man with the best hand before the draw has the best chance to win the hand and so wants to increase the amount of money in the pot. However, George has no way of knowing that his pair of kings is the best hand, so he simply calls the previous bet.

Harry has a pair of tens. He reasons that one or both of the previous bettors (Dick and George) has at least a higher pair, so the odds are against him. Thus, Harry drops with his pair of tens. Nice play, Harry. You have avoided the temptation of hoping to win with a known inferior hand.

The betting now has gone completely around the table

but the betting round is not completed because the bets are not equalized. Al, Bob, and Charlie are still active but have not matched the $1 bet by Dick. (Remember, these three players had checked at their first betting opportunity.)

So the betting goes back to Al. Al has an **open-ended four straight**. This means he has four cards in sequence (7-6-5-4) with the possibility of adding a card at either end to turn his holding into a straight. (Compare this with Frank's holding of Q-J-9-8 which was an **inside four straight** and fillable only with a 10.) Al figures he has two ways to win, and makes a speculative (not recommended) call of the $1 bet.

Bob and Charlie both drop, so the bets have been equalized with Dick, George, and Al having bet $1 each. The pot now contains $5 ($2 of antes and $3 of first-round bets). The betting on the first round can be summarized as follows:

(dealer)

AL	BOB	CHARLIE	DICK	ED	FRANK	GEORGE	HARRY
* Check	Check	Check	Bet($1)	*Drop*	*Drop*	Call($1)	*Drop*
Call($1)	*Drop*	*Drop*					

* Eldest hand

With the first betting round completed, the active players have earned the right to draw cards and attempt to improve their hands. The underlined cards are the ones discarded by the active players:

Al	♥ J	♠ 7	♥ 6	♣ 5	♠ 4
Dick	♦ Q̲	♣ Q	♥ 7̲	♦ 6̲	♠ 2̲
George	♠ A	♣ K	♠ K̲	♣ 9̲	♣ 7̲

Al draws the ♦ 5, giving him a pair of fives; Dick draws ♠ J, ♦ 9, ♥ 8, leaving him with a pair of queens; George draws ♠ 10, ♥ 4, ♦ 2, leaving him with a pair of kings.

Draw Poker

The active players are now ready for the second betting round. Although Al is the first active player on the dealer's left, Dick is the first bettor in the second betting round *because he bet first (opened) in the previous betting round.*

Dick checks. It is a new betting round, so it is possible to check if no other player has bet. Dick has not improved his pair of queens and has no reason to try to increase the stake. George also checks. He must be wary of Al, who is sitting behind him. George remembers that Al drew one card and thus was probably one card away from a very good hand. George therefore refuses to commit himself until he sees what action Al takes.

Al also checks. He knows he does not have the highest hand and a bet on his part would be in the nature of a bluff—a false display of strength—hoping the other players will think he has made a straight or flush with his one-card draw. Al thinks such a bluff will probably not work against two opponents, so he cuts his losses by checking out the betting round. The second round of betting is now equalized (no player having bet), and that means it is time for the showdown.

George, with a pair of kings, has the highest-ranking hand and wins the pot.

Two observations are in order.

First, this hand would have been played in a small fraction of the time it took you to read about it. An experienced player would require no more than a second for any decision that arose. As you gain poker experience, you will find that many actions gradually become automatic.

Second, this was a routine deal, relatively dull as deals go. It would have been misleading to present a wildly exciting deal in the sample. Many hands of draw poker will be just as routine as the one we have just watched. But it is the garden-variety deal which largely determines the winners and losers at the poker table. Making correct decisions in the majority of routine situations will win you far more money than the occasional spectacular bluff or the once in a lifetime that you are dealt a straight flush. There will be enough interesting poker hands to satisfy even the most demanding. But there will not be enough to make up for careless play on the ordinary deals.

SUMMARY

Let's have a quick summary of the different stages of draw poker and their essential features:

(1) Deal—five cards to each player (all cards concealed).

(2) First betting round—eldest hand (to left of dealer) speaks first.

(3) Draw—eldest hand first; never deal bottom card; reshuffle previous discards if necessary.

(4) Second betting round—opener (first bettor in previous betting round) speaks first.

(5) Showdown—all active hands exposed.

DRAW POKER VARIATIONS

It would take a complete volume to list every version of draw poker, no less to give pointers on how to win, but there are several variations of the basic game which enjoy wide popularity. As you are fairly likely to run into one or more of these variations even if your poker travels are not extensive, I will give the rules for these games.

(1) **Jackpots.** This game is sometimes called "jacks or

better to open," which description tells the whole story. The only change from the usual rules of draw poker is that the opener must have at least as good a hand as a pair of jacks to open the betting. (After the hand is opened, anything goes.)

There is no requirement for the opener to keep the values which legalized his initial bet (these values are often called **openers**) and, to avoid arguments in those cases in which the opener may have thrown away part or all of his openers, the cards discarded by the first bettor should be placed face down in the center of the pot. Notice that this must be done on *every* deal, not only when opener actually does break up his hand in the draw, for it would be a disadvantage to be forced to announce whether or not the opening values were kept.

When a hand is passed out at jackpots (as will happen more often than in ordinary draw poker), the deal passes to the left and generally another round of antes is paid to the pot.

Variations of jackpots include **acepots** (in which opener needs a pair of aces or better) and **progressive jackpots** (if a deal is not opened when a pair of jacks is required, the next deal requires a pair of queens to open, and so forth). These versions both have the drawback that too much time is spent dealing the cards and too little playing poker, for with the increased requirements many more deals will be passed out.

(2) **Straight draw poker.** This variation eliminates the check as a possible action on the first round of betting. In other words, each player must bet or drop when his turn comes on the first betting round.

(3) **Blind and straddle.** This game is sometimes called **blind opening**, and again the name is a good description. To

avoid passed-out hands, the eldest hand is required to open the betting automatically. This is called a blind opening because the player bets without looking at his hand. In some variations there is an automatic (blind) raise by the next player, called a **straddle**. Some games allow any number of straddles (raises without looking at one's cards).

It goes without saying that each of these variations requires adjustments in a winning player's strategy. This is true of any of the myriad variations of modern poker. In the next chapter, we will consider how one should go about mastering the different forms of poker.

QUIZ

In each of the draw poker deals described below, our eight friends are sitting around the table clockwise in alphabetical order of first names. Harry is the dealer with Al on his left (see diagram, page 36).

For each deal, construct a betting chart for the first round of betting. The stakes: ante twenty-five cents ($2 paid by the dealer); bet before the draw, $1; bet after the draw, $2.

After constructing the charts, answer these questions about each deal:
(a) How much money is in the pot after the first betting round?
(b) What were the sources of the money in the pot?
(c) Which player will act first in the second betting round?
(d) Which players are still active?

Deal One

Al and Bob check; Charlie opens; Dick calls; Ed and Frank drop; George raises; Harry drops; Al calls; Bob drops; Charlie reraises; Dick drops; George calls; Al drops.

Draw Poker

Deal Two

Al checks; Bob opens; Charlie and Dick drop; Ed calls; Frank raises; George drops; Harry calls; Al drops; Bob drops; Ed calls.

SOLUTIONS

Deal One

AL	BOB	CHARLIE	DICK	ED	FRANK	GEORGE	HARRY (dealer)
* Check	Check	Bet($1)	Call($1)	*Drop*	*Drop*	Raise($2)	*Drop*
Call($2)	*Drop*	Raise($2)	*Drop*			Call($1)	
Drop							

* Eldest hand

(a) The pot has $11.
(b) Ante: $2. Al: $2. Charlie: $3. Dick: $1. George: $3.
(c) Charlie, the opener, who is still an active player.
(d) Charlie and George. Al and Dick have contributed money to the pot, but no longer have a chance to win as they failed to meet the amout bet by other players.

Deal Two

AL	BOB	CHARLIE	DICK	ED	FRANK	GEO.	HARRY (dealer)
* Check	Bet($1)	*Drop*	*Drop*	Call($1)	Raise($2)	*Drop*	Call ($2)
Drop	*Drop*			Call($1)			

* Eldest hand

(a) The pot has $9.
(b) Ante: $2. Bob: $1. Ed, Frank, and Harry: $2 each.
(c) Ed. Bob, the opener, is no longer an active player. Ed is the first active player to the left of Bob.
(d) Ed, Frank, and Harry.

43

◎ ◎ ◎ ◎ ◎

THREE

How to Learn Poker

Thus far we have learned the rules common to all forms of poker and the mechanics of one specific game—draw poker. The next logical step would seem to be a study of winning procedures at draw poker.

And so it is. Nonetheless, for fear that an immediate introduction to battle conditions will tempt you to enter the fray without a proper grounding in fundamentals, I will digress for two chapters.

In this chapter, I present an overall plan for your poker education. You will learn little about the game itself in this chapter, but its contents will enable you to make better use of later acquisitions.

In Chapter Four, I will introduce the elements of winning poker strategy—those considerations which should play a part in determining your poker decisions *regardless of the form of the game being played.* I have withheld this vital information until draw poker had been explained and thus was available as a source of illustration. I precede it with this chapter so that you will be in a position to make good use of this crucial knowledge.

How to Learn Poker

Let us therefore turn our attention to your approach to learning poker: where you should look for poker information and what you should do with it once you have found it.

THE THREE ASPECTS OF POKER LEARNING

Your poker knowledge and maturity will derive from three sources: instruction, observation, experience. Paradoxically, while these phases of your poker education occur logically in the order shown, their order of importance is in reverse. Thus, your *poker experience*—what you gain from actual participation in real-life poker games—will be more valuable than anything else you can learn. The next best thing to playing is watching. Therefore, *observation* is next most important. At the bottom of the list is your *poker instruction*—what you learn about poker by reading books, asking questions of experienced players, listening to others discuss the game.

The paradox is that although playing is more valuable than watching, one cannot play effectively without first having observed intelligently. Similarly, one can gain little from observation unless one has been instructed beforehand on what to look for.

To apply the above information to your poker career is easy. You need beware only of jumping into poker games too quickly. At some point during your poker education you may experience a surge of confidence. Use restraint. Walk—don't run. Prefer continuing an orderly development of your understanding to leaping into action immediately. In the end, you will win more.

On the other hand, once you have arrived at the stage where you are playing poker regularly, and are analyzing your skills from the point of view of actual poker experience, remember that *nothing substitutes for practical experience.*

Suppose, for example, that you read somewhere in this book that "Method A is good strategy; Method B is poor strategy." Being a good pupil and having enjoyed the book, you quite naturally have adopted Method A. Suppose, however, that you have kept track of the results obtained with Method A and also those obtained with Method B (possibly by others in your group) and have discovered that better results are obtained with Method B. Is this just a freakish run of luck or was my advice misguided?

Assuming your experience covers a large sampling of deals, the rule that nothing substitutes for experience indicates that my advice was not applicable to your situation. How is it that I give such advice in this book and try to palm myself off as an expert on the subject? Each and every poker game has its own peculiarities. Many groups have similar characteristics, but no two are identical. No one can possibly have experienced all the different characteristics of all the different poker games all over the world. Thus, the best one can do when giving advice is to state which stratagems will succeed in *most* games.

At any rate, it is clear that on occasion, advice that would be sound under "standard" conditions *will not apply to a particular situation or a particular poker group.*

And now you can see why nothing can substitute for experience. Because so much of poker depends on "local conditions," you must be prepared to modify anything and everything you have learned when necessary to meet the needs of a particular poker situation. This is not to say that you should throw away your "book larnin'" on a moment's notice. On the contrary, the rejection of established poker strategy should be the exception rather than the rule. But unless you are flexible enough to know when to break the rules, you will never win as much as you should.

An absurd illustration may clarify this point. Suppose you are blessed with the following poker hand:

◆K   ◆Q   ◆J   ◆10   ◆9.

This is one of the highest-ranking hands, being a king-high straight flush. You will lose the pot only if another player has a royal flush in spades, hearts, or clubs. The odds against an opponent holding such a hand are approximately 850,000 to 1. Not a bad situation for you to be in! If your opponent bets the limit of, say, one dollar, I recommend you raise him to two dollars. Not even the Sad Sack should lose this hand.

Now let us alter the circumstances. Suppose the rules are such that any amount may be bet. One of your opponents is a highly conservative player. His income is about $7500 a year before taxes and in your experience he has never bet more than $10 in any one pot. There you are, sitting with

◆K   ◆Q   ◆J   ◆10   ◆9

and this conservative opponent suddenly bets $20,000!

Would you say it is still 850,000 to 1 against his holding a royal flush? Of course not. In fact, like it or not, you know deep down inside that a king-high straight flush just may not be enough to win this pot. It may be the best hand you have ever held, but the correct play is to *drop*.

No poker book is going to tell you to drop out when the odds are 850,000 to 1 in your favor. Yet, if the circumstances are extreme enough—such as in the fantasy I have just presented—it can be the correct play.

And that is why I say you should build your poker knowledge carefully, yet must be prepared to reject standard techniques on the basis of experience within your own poker circle. Thus, some of my advice will be on the subject of when to forget other advice.

PUTTING THE BOOKS TO WORK

Getting down to cases, how can you best take advantage of this book and other sources of poker knowledge?

1. Poker instruction.

Begin your poker instruction with basic textbooks. Your first step should be to master the rules. I judge that 50 percent of all poker players do not confidently know the correct ranking of the hands. My estimate, conservative by most standards, is that fewer than 10 percent of all players know the correct rules *of the forms of poker they play.*

You certainly don't want to be one of the crowd. A thorough knowledge of the rules is essential to winning poker. Does this mean that at most 10 percent of all poker players are winners? Yes. In fact, no more than 5 percent win significantly (in proportion to the stakes of their games). The other 95 percent are not all losers: many break about even and a few are small winners. Nonetheless, uncounted millions are losers because of an improper understanding of the rules.

It's a silly reason to lose. It isn't even fun.

Having firmly grasped the rules of the forms of poker you intend to play, your next move is to continue reading about poker strategy. Here another question arises. Opinions on correct poker technique vary. Should you stick with the views of one author or should you get different points of view?

Part of the answer to this question is financial. If you are reading this book because you find poker intellectually stimulating and you want to learn more about it, and/or you play poker for but small stakes, this book should satisfy your curiosity as well as keep your pocket lined with pennies. On the other hand, if you intend to play poker for sizable stakes, it would be the height of *mathematical* folly not to invest a few more dollars and read as many poker books as you can find. By doing so, you will have an opportunity to compare this book with others. In many cases, you will find my views in agreement with other authors'. It is fairly safe to accept these pronouncements as "the real McCoy." On the other hand, there are topics on which opinion is divided. You should mark these for special attention, compare the views of different authors and examine their reasoning, and, most important, make a mental note *to be guided by your own experience in these debatable areas.*

Why do I describe this situation as mathematical? Because the amount of money that will depend on one or two decisions in your poker game may far outweigh the price of any books you might buy. Imagine not buying a book for, say, five dollars, and losing a ten-dollar pot because you missed out on some tactical point presented in that book. Could anything be more humiliating?

2. *Poker observation.*

After you have read a few poker books, you should summarize the essential points. You need not go so far as to underline important sentences but you might well make yourself a list of the things you consider most important.

Your first battle, however, will be from the sidelines. You will be faced with the death-defying task of watching a poker game (the one you hope to play in would be best, for reasons that will appear later) and trying to understand it.

After you have watched long enough to feel confident that you understand what is going on (this may happen almost immediately or it may take several sessions), you then face an even more difficult job. You must now try to relate what is happening in the game to what has been discussed in this book. In particular, you should look for illustrations of the general principles discussed in the next chapter.

In the course of your watching, it is likely that some events will occur which you do not fully understand. If you cannot relate these situations to anything you have learned to that point, try asking one of the players in the game— preferably a winner.

3. *Poker experience.*

Eventually the urge to play will be too great to restrain and you will get your feet wet. The chances are that no matter how diligently you have done your homework, you will lose at the outset. Do not be discouraged. *This is to be expected and is part of your poker education.* (Do remember, however, to budget for such losses.) If you are a consistent winner at the very beginning of your poker career, you don't need this or any other book. (In fact, how about sending *me* a copy of *yours?*)

So you lose. What should you do about it? Take advantage of it, of course. Sit down and analyze the reasons for your defeat. Keep track of your losing situations. Try to understand them in terms of the principles discussed in this book. On this basis, attempt to correct your mistakes.

After you have played for a while, you should be able to eliminate losses caused by inexperience. From this point on, your poker career may move in one of two directions. The favorable one is steady improvement, presumably caused by your own analysis of losses and correction of basic errors. Should you see this occur (a tipoff would be that you recognize yourself doing things "right" that you previously did "wrong") you are then ready to become a winner at the poker table. We'll return to this in Chapter Twelve.

The other possibility is a grim one. You do not improve. You continue to lose. If this process continues over a period of time, and the situation is unabated when you attempt to analyze your losses and correct your errors, there are several courses of action open to you.

1. Start the learning process over again. It is possible that you moved too hastily in your pursuit of the mastering of poker. Go more slowly than necessary to make sure you do not fall into the same trap again.

2. Find a different poker game. One of the possibilities is that the game you are playing in is too strong for you. It is no disgrace to seek easier competition—most players do at one time or another, either by switching to another poker group or inviting new players.

3. If neither of the above solutions is satisfactory, and if your enjoyment in playing does not make up for the monetary losses you incur, your only recourse is to stop playing. (If you are under social pressure to play, take up card tricks and perform one at every possible moment. Soon you will no longer be invited.)

Above all, you must avoid the error of blaming your poker losses on poor luck. This attitude is certain to lead to continued bad results. *For poker is almost entirely a game of skill.* There are few games, and virtually no gambling games, in which the importance of skill is greater than in poker.

Therefore, if you continue to lose, it is because others in the game are better players. Your techniques are not as good as theirs. Blaming your losses on circumstances is not the way to change your "luck" from bad to good.

F O U R

◎ ◎ ◎ ◎ ◎

Basic Principles of Poker

The advice presented in this chapter is applicable to all forms of poker. The examples used to illustrate various points will be based on the "typical" poker group we have created—eight players, draw poker, quarter ante, bet limit one dollar before the draw and two dollars after the draw—but the principles apply to all forms of poker.

No inference should be drawn as to the relative importance of the six topics because of the order of presentation. None is any more or less important than the others. All are essential parts of the game of poker. I have placed first those topics which seemed to me to stand by themselves better than the others.

MONEY MANAGEMENT

Poker is a money game. Other games can survive the lack of a gambling element—indeed, some are better without it—but poker holds little interest if this facet is removed.

It follows that a successful poker player must have good gambling habits. And this makes it logical to discuss money. "Money management" is a term often applied to gambling, and to poker in particular. I use the term here in a restricted sense. What I mean by "money management" is organization of capital and the adjustment of risks. I consider this definition restricted because many writers include what I call "poker overhead" (page 66) under the heading of "money management." I consider the distinction worthwhile, for poker overhead is a subject best considered at the poker table while the planning of money management (under my definition) should be done beforehand.

Everyone who plays poker *hopes* to win. But some players *expect* to lose and this in itself puts them at a disadvantage. Superior poker strategy calls for backing your hand to the hilt when favorable situations arise. Poker being a game of percentages, following the best poker strategy will occasionally produce a considerable loss—either on a specific deal or even for a session. Every so often a long shot must win. *A player who fears this type of loss cannot take proper advantage of his winning situations. He is automatically a losing player.*

Proper money management will avoid this problem. In order to avoid being in fear of loss, you must adjust your risks *before you start playing.* Capital allotments should be made for a period of poker play (say a year) as well as for each individual session. In order to have these limits accomplish their purpose of avoiding the fear of loss *they must never be violated.* If you have lost your established limit, either for a session or for a year, *stop playing!*

No doubt you will have observed that setting these limits will also prevent a painful financial loss. It would be foolish to state that this byproduct is anything but beneficial. However, from our present viewpoint, this gain is only an incidental one. We are concerned with money management as an essential of winning poker.

It is foolish not to avoid losing more than you can afford. It is also unsound poker to worry about this while you are playing. So the formula for successful money management is:

Before playing, prepare for potential losses and set your limit.

While playing, think only about winning.

So much for the theory of money management. How do we put it into practice?

It goes without saying that everyone must set his own limits. It may be helpful to think of the figure budgeted for "overall poker expenses" (this figure, by the way, should include transportation and incidental expenses) as part of the money you set aside each year for entertainment and relaxation. For an evening's enjoyment, you pay a certain amount to see a movie or a show or a ball game. Think of poker in the same terms: What amount are you prepared to pay for such-and-such number of sessions of enjoyment at the poker table? Come up with a sensible and honest answer to this question, and you have probably chosen your overall limit wisely.

While your overall poker limit depends largely on your own personal situation, your stake for an individual session must be guided by other factors. It is impractical not to leave yourself a certain leeway within any one session. It would be foolish to have a session limit so low that one or two early reverses would send you home early in the evening. If you find, however, that a practical session limit exceeds 10 percent of your yearly allotment, the stakes are too high for you. If you cannot bear to play in a lower-stake game, I recommend you cut down your number of sessions. There are other activities which are almost as worthwhile as playing poker—reading a good poker book, for example—and you can spend some time at these pursuits. The purpose of cutting down is the avoidance of the situation in which you have insufficient capital to back your efforts, which in turn leads to the fear of losses while playing.

However good a player you are, this situation will always impair your judgment and consequently lower your chances of winning.

Unfortunately, it is almost impossible to offer precise advice on how much money one should sit down with in a given game. The temperament of the game has a considerable effect on the speed with which money changes hands. A conservative game with a dollar limit might be equivalent to a loose game with a quarter limit. I'll make an educated guess for our sample game (eight-player draw poker, quarter ante, one dollar and two dollar betting limits) which you can apply to your own game by comparing the stakes. Assuming the players in our sample game to be typical, reasonably conservative players, so that raises occur only every so often and reraises less frequently, I would say that fifty dollars should be enough "backing" as a session limit and should probably ensure satisfactory flexibility.

Of course, if the players are more aggressive in your game than those described above, more capital will be needed. Here it is impossible to give specific advice except for one tip. When discussing your poker development (Chapter Three), I mentioned that it would be a good idea to pick the game you hope to play in as the game you watch. One reason for this is that by watching your own game, you will get a good idea of the true nature of the stakes; you will see how much money usually changes hands during the course of an evening. This information will help you set your session limit intelligently.

Changes in your personal situation may cause changes in

the loss limits you establish, but once established, these limits should be inviolable. That is the secret of money management.

Why is money management, which might seem better placed in a book on home economics than one on poker, so important to successful play? The answer is that unless you are a hardened professional gambler you will play less effectively when you are losing. Thus, it is *essential* for you to drop out of the game once you have lost your limit. Also, if this limit is not realistic, and you allow yourself the possibility of losing more than you can afford, you will be *worrying* so much about losing that the effect will be as detrimental as if you actually were losing.

I have little doubt that my advice on money management will be the most difficult to follow of all the suggestions in this book. Yet, for most players, it is possibly the most important.

THE FUNDAMENTAL PRINCIPLE OF BETTING

Poker is gambling. Gambling involves taking chances whether we call it a bet (on a horse race) or an investment (in the stock market) or by any other name. There is a fundamental principle which applies to taking chances and therefore to betting in poker.

Let's look first at an example. Suppose you are betting on a game which involves dice. Each die has six faces, labeled from one to six, and we will presume that the die is weighted so that each number has an equal chance to appear when the die is thrown. You bet a nickel that the number six will be thrown. If six is not thrown, you lose your nickel; if six comes up, however, you win a quarter. You are making a *fair bet*. Why? *Because the odds against winning the game are the same as the betting odds.* There are five other numbers besides six which can be thrown. Therefore, it is 5 to 1 against your winning the game. As you are also receiving 5 to 1 on your money (twenty-five cents to five cents), your bet is fair. Although if the game is played only once you cannot come out even (you must be either plus twenty-five cents or minus five cents), in the long run, if the game is played many times, you will theoretically wind up with no profit or loss.

Suppose you played the same game, but were paid only a dime when a six was thrown. Your bet is now a poor one, for the betting odds (only 2 to 1) are *lower* than the odds against winning (still 5 to 1). This would be an *unfavorable* bet. On the other hand, if you were paid a half-dollar when the six came through, the betting odds would be 10 to 1, *higher* than the odds against winning of 5 to 1, and the bet would be a *good* one.

The soundness of all bets can be judged in this way. A bet is *favorable* if the betting odds are *higher* than the odds against winning, *fair* (break-even) if the betting odds are about *equal* to the odds against winning, and *unfavorable* if the betting odds are *lower* than the odds against winning. The essence of winning poker is to make favorable bets and avoid unfavorable bets. If you do nothing more than avoid losing betting situations, even if you never bluff successfully and your psychology is mediocre, *you will never do worse than break even at poker.*

Except for that very rare sure thing, even the most favorable bets will lose once in a while. The reason that the better players always win at poker over a period of time is that there are enough opportunities for the true odds to make themselves felt. If you continue to make favorable bets, even though you will lose some of them, you will be a winner in the end.

GAUGING THE ODDS

It follows that it is a basic poker skill to judge what the odds are: first, against your winning of the pot in question; second, the betting odds you are being offered. The first is a complicated question, and cannot always be computed exactly. The second is straightforward. However, it is important to avoid the fallacious reasoning that plagues well over half of all poker players: *the fallacy that money you previously placed into the pot affects your present odds.* Every bet you make in a poker game should be considered as a separate entity. Your previous betting, however sound or unsound it may have been *at that time,* has no effect whatsoever on the present odds offered by the pot (i.e. the betting odds).

The simplest example of this principle in action involves the ante. We saw previously that it makes no difference whether each of eight players antes a quarter or whether the dealer puts up the entire two dollars. Similarly, for purposes of computing the "pot odds" it suffices to count the antes (in this case) as two dollars in the pot. *It makes no difference how the two dollars got there.*

Here are some examples of how the pot odds are computed. Let's go back to our eight-player game of draw poker. Harry deals, putting in the total ante of $2. Al opens (for $1). Bob, Charlie, Dick, Ed, Frank, and George all drop. It's now up to Harry. What are his pot odds? Harry is called upon to put $1 into the pot. Therefore, his potential loss by calling Al's bet is $1. On the other hand, his potential gain is the amount of money now in the pot, which is $3 ($2 from the antes, $1 bet by Al). The pot odds are 3 to 1, and if Harry thinks the odds against him at this stage are no more than 3 to 1, he has a favorable bet by calling Al's $1. Nowhere in this calculation did we use the fact that it was Harry himself who put the ante into the pot—the result would be the same if someone else had been the dealer.

That shows how half the battle of the odds is accomplished. The other half is somewhat more difficult. Skill in determination of the odds against winning usually comes only with great experience. Nonetheless, even a relative beginner can handle some of the basic cases. To begin, let's take an oversimplified (and highly impractical) example. Let's say that Al and Harry have come early and while waiting for the other players to gather they decide to play some "straight" poker (no draw). Each antes fifty cents per hand and the bet limit is $1. On the first hand, Harry deals and Al decides to bet $1 without looking at his five cards. Harry, being more conservative, looks at his hand and sees he holds:

♠A　　♥Q　　♥10　　♦2　　♣2

Should Harry call Al's $1 bet?

The pot odds (betting odds) are easy to calculate. The pot now has $2 ($1 from the antes, $1 bet by Al). Harry must risk $1 to call Al's bet, but stands to win the $2 in the pot. The pot odds are 2 to 1.

Now what are the odds against Harry winning? Al has not looked at his cards, so we gain no information from the fact that he has made a bet. Al will win if he has a pair or better, for Harry has the lowest possible pair. What is the chance that Al has a pair? I mentioned in Chapter One that approximately half of all poker hands have no pair. Therefore, it is even money that Al has a pair. Since the odds against Harry winning are even (1 to 1) and the pot odds are *higher* (2 to 1), it is favorable for Harry if he calls Al's bet.

Remember the process: compute the pot odds (betting odds); compute the odds against your winning; make the bet if the pot odds are *higher* than the odds against winning.

Let's apply this technique in some practical poker situations. Again we follow Harry, who is now the dealer in the eight-handed draw poker game. He places the total $2 ante in the pot, deals the cards, and finds that he has dealt himself:

♠J   ♠9   ♠8   ♠6   ♥2

Al opens for $1; all the others drop out. Should Harry call the bet?

Once again, it is easy to determine the pot odds. By calling, Harry risks $1. He stands to win the $3 in the pot ($2 in antes, $1 bet by Al). Thus, the pot offers Harry odds of 3 to 1.*

What is Harry's chance to win the pot? Clearly Al must have something better than jack-high (the present value of Harry's hand) to open the betting, so Harry's best chance to win the pot is to discard the deuce of hearts, hoping to draw a spade to complete a flush. This would be a very high-ranking hand, and we may assume that if Harry is lucky enough to fill his flush that he will win the pot. What is the chance that Harry will draw a spade?

---

* These odds are actually a bit higher, for by calling he retains a chance to win more money from Al after the draw. But he also may lose more by attempting to win more, so this calculation is a bit too complex for the present stage of our investigation.

Basic Principles of Poker

From Harry's viewpoint, the card he draws to replace the deuce of hearts can be any of the 47 cards he does not see. Nine of these cards are spades; 38 are not spades. Therefore, the odds against Harry drawing a spade (and thus the odds against his winning the pot) are 38 to 9, or slightly higher than 4 to 1.

Our job is now done. The pot odds are 3 to 1; the odds against Harry winning are above 4 to 1. The pot odds are *not* higher; thus, the bet is *not* favorable. Harry should *drop!*

Let's look at the other side of the coin. Same situation; same hand for Harry. But now Bob and Charlie call Al's bet of $1 before the rest drop out. What should Harry do now? Even with three players against him Harry should still expect to win if he draws his flush. So the odds against his winning are still slightly over 4 to 1. But the pot now offers odds of 5 to 1 ($2 from antes, $3 from bets). Since the pot odds are now *higher* than the odds against winning, Harry should *call* and try to draw his flush. In the long run (though not necessarily on any one specific deal) he will be a winner by doing so.

Paradoxically, although Harry's chance of winning is (slightly) reduced when more players are competing against him, the same bet becomes favorable where previously it was unfavorable. This emphasizes the nature of the fundamental principle of betting as a *comparison* of the odds against winning with the odds offered by the pot.

Like everything else, the basic principle of betting is open to exceptions. For example, suppose someone offers to bet you on the toss of a coin. (We assume the coin is known to be fair—let's say it is your own coin.) If the coin comes up heads, he will pay you $1050; if it comes up tails you will pay him "only" $1000. This is a "good" bet for you, since the betting odds are *above* 1 to 1 and the odds against winning are exactly 1 to 1. But who wants to risk $1000 on the toss of a coin?

One final warning applies both to poker and to betting in general. The basic principle assumes that you can compute the odds precisely, or at least close to it. A different principle draws attention to the fact that it is very important to be certain you have all the information necessary to compute the odds properly. This admonishment is called the "jack of spades principle." It goes like this: if someone offers to bet you that he can snap his fingers and make the jack of spades jump out of a deck of cards and spit in your eye, *don't bet*. Rest assured that if you make the bet you are in for an eyeful.

Here are a couple of classic swindles which indicate that you will do well to protect yourself against overapplying the basic principle out of your league. One involves a well-known trickster with considerable golfing ability who, finding himself with some spare time in Chicago one wintry evening, offered to bet one of his "pigeons" a considerable amount that he could drive a golf ball more than a mile! His customer, undoubtedly thinking the offer was a drunken boast, rapidly put up the stake. The swindler promptly took his golfing gear out to Lake Michigan (which happened to be frozen over), put his back to the wind, teed up, and took a mighty swing. The sucker didn't even bother to measure.

The other maneuver is one which will enable you to lose friends right in your own living room. Tear an ordinary paper match out of a book and mark an X on one side. Offer to throw the match up and pay fifty cents if the X side comes up, but to collect only a quarter if the unmarked side shows. Your opponent will undoubtedly smell a rat, so you tell him that to even out the odds you will collect one dollar if the match should happen to land on its edge. He will probably agree to this (while mentally lowering his estimation of your intelligence). Bend the match in half before you throw it and hold out a hand for your dollar.

POKER MATHEMATICS

Many people are under the impression that poker involves highly complicated mathematical calculations and that one cannot be a successful player without considerable mathematical ability. They are both right and wrong. Poker does involve abstruse mathematics. But for the most part, these considerations play no part in determining the winner at the poker table. Even the greatest poker experts are largely unaware of the mathematics of poker; or, if they are aware of it, they disregard it. And rightly so, for two reasons. First, complicated mathematical figuring is important only on rare occasions. Second, on those infrequent occasions when one could make use of high-level calculation to obtain a precise answer, an approximate answer will serve equally well.

So I advise you not to worry about mathematics in your poker playing. True, you must know some of the basic odds, but I undertake to do these computations for you and let you know the answers. What you *should* know about poker mathematics is the *type* of situation that is subject to mathematical analysis, as opposed to a purely psychological consideration.

There are three phases of poker knowledge which depend on mathematics: the basic value of a hand, the odds against improving a hand, the raising principle.

A. THE BASIC VALUE OF A HAND

The basic value of a hand depends on the chances of a higher-valued hand being held by an opponent. This is a mathematical fact, and although you should certainly not delve into exact probabilities, you should have a good idea of what constitutes a poor hand, a fair hand, a good hand, and an excellent hand, in each form of poker you intend to play. Thus, when it comes time to give pointers on winning strategy in different forms of poker, I will present hand values—the normal values required to bet and raise, the average winning hand, and so on. These values are intended to serve *not* as a guide to playing, but as a base point from which to start your calculation.

The value table is useful only as a base point because *all values vary with circumstances.* On page 47, I gave an example of a hand which was an 850,000-to-1 favorite to win the pot. Yet, circumstances dictated a *drop* because it was about 10 million-to-1 that your opponent held a better hand. Similarly, in our sample game of draw poker, if you start with a pair of aces, *in normal circumstances* you have a good hand. But if there is a raise or two before the draw, you probably have an inferior hand.

To be able to adjust his hand valuation with the circumstances is the mark of the superior poker player. But one must have a starting point before any adjustment can take place. Therefore, one of the musts when learning a new form of poker is to determine how good various hands are. Since this will depend both on mathematical probabilities *and* on the tendencies of the players involved (what might be a moderate hand in a conservative game might be a fine hand against free-wheeling players), you must combine book learning and observation and play experience to determine the value of hands in your own game.

B. THE ODDS AGAINST IMPROVING

To apply the fundamental principle of betting, one must know both the pot odds and the odds against winning. The pot odds are easily determined by counting the pot and considering the amount of the bet. To know the odds against winning, you must be able to determine the chance that you and/or your opponents will improve your hands (through drawing, for example).

It is difficult and bothersome to work out the percentages while playing—your thinking is better directed along other lines—so there is no alternative to memorizing several basic odds against improvement. These will be presented later (Chapter Five and elsewhere). Do not dismiss them lightly as being boring. (Unless, of course, you don't like winning.)

C. THE "RAISING PRINCIPLE"

The "raising principle" is a corollary to the fundamental principle of betting. It is so obvious after explanation that one wonders how anyone cannot be aware of it. Yet, I doubt that one poker player in twenty fully understands and makes use of it. It is simply this: *a raise lowers the odds offered by the pot.*

Let's review some of the situations previously discussed. In our eight-handed game, on page 60, Al opened for $1 and the next six players dropped. The pot offered Harry 3 to 1 on a call ($3 to $1) but it offers only 3 to 2 (or 1½ to 1) on a raise, for Harry must put in $2 to try to win $3. (One can argue that this raise will require Al to put in another $1, giving Harry $4 to $2, but that is not correct reasoning. First of all, if Al calls the raise, Harry must revise his estimate of winning chances for Al will have a better hand; for another thing, Harry is left open to a *reraise* by Al.) Harry held a **four flush** (one card away from a flush) and had odds against winning of a bit over 4 to 1, so he properly dropped out.

On page 61, Al's opening bet was called by Bob and Charlie, so Harry was offered 5-to-1 odds by the pot and he properly stayed in, risking $1 to win $5 on the chance of drawing a flush. Many players would incorrectly decide that since Harry's betting odds were favorable he should *raise,* not merely call.

But this is not so, since by raising, Harry would cut the odds offered by the pot from 5 to 1 to 2½ to 1. Since odds of 2½ to 1 would not justify playing on what is roughly a 4-to-1 chance against winning, Harry's hand is worth a call *but not a raise.*

The main point here is to avoid the trap of thinking that what is a good call is necessarily a good raise. A separate computation should be made, and the fundamental principle applied, to determine whether or not you should raise.

POKER OVERHEAD

Poker technique includes both skill and style. Thus far, we have discussed mostly skill and technique. Now let's turn for a moment to poker style.

Although distinctions can be made between the mode of play of any two poker players, almost every player will fall into one of two general categories. For convenience, let's call these the "bulls" and the "bears."

The first group—the bulls—consists of players who like a lot of action. The bulls raise frequently; they refuse to be shut out of a pot when they have moderate values; they are in a large number of hands at the showdown—both winning and losing large numbers of pots; money passes in and out of their hands quickly; they are aggressive. The bears are cautious; they prefer to wait for a good hand and then try to build the pot, rather than speculate on doubtful values; they play in fewer hands than the bulls; they reach fewer showdowns and win few pots during a session; they also lose money in fewer pots; they are conservative.

There are, of course, many degrees of bullishness and bearishness. Even taking this into account, which style of play—bull or bear—is more effective?

The answer is that it depends. And that brings us to the matter of poker overhead. The ante represents the overhead in your "poker business." It is the amount of rent you must pay to keep your store open, i.e., it is the fee required for the right to sit at the table, be dealt cards, and have an opportunity to make bets and attempt to win the pot. The most important factors in determining whether bullish or bearish style will be more successful are the tendencies of the other players in the game and *the ratio of the ante to the betting limit.*

The second consideration is a fixed thing, and therefore it is easier to start our analysis there. Other factors being equal, it is preferable to be bullish when the ante is high compared with the betting limit. Taking an outrageous example for emphasis, suppose that in our familiar eight-handed draw-poker game, with betting limits of $1 before the draw and $2 after the draw, the (total) ante is $8 ($1 per player) instead of $2 (twenty-five cents per player). Since each pot starts with $8, when it comes time to decide whether or not to throw in your $1, the odds offered by the pot will be tremendous. Who wouldn't want to risk $1, even on a long shot, for a chance to win $11 or $12? On the other hand, suppose now that the ante is only forty cents (five cents per player). You now need considerably better values to risk betting, for the odds offered by the pot are comparatively low. The amount you stand to gain is small compared with the amount you must bet.

Here is a brief chart showing the effect of the different

rates of ante on the pot odds. In each case, the listed odds are those offered by the pot to a player who is considering calling an opening bet of $1 before the draw.

Ante (total)	Pot odds if only opener has bet	Pot odds if one other player has called opener's bet
$8	9 to 1	10 to 1
$2 (normal)	3 to 1	4 to 1
forty cents	1.4 to 1	2.4 to 1

You can see from this chart that the effect of a high ante will be to encourage speculation while the effect of a low ante will be to stifle betting. Unquestionably, this factor should suggest a guideline for establishing the ratio of ante to betting limit in your own game. My own recommendation, used in our sample game, is to have the total ante equal to twice the betting limit before the draw. (The exact amounts involved do not affect the issue. These will vary with the financial status of the players.)

Restating the effect of a high or low ante in terms of poker style: if the ante is relatively high, one should be a bull. Otherwise, the high cost of the ante will mount up over the large number of hands which you do not enter and it will be impossible to win even if you do very well on the hands you play. On the other hand, when the ante is low, one should be a bear, for there is not enough in the pot to make speculation worthwhile.

Therefore, as a practical guide, loosen up your play (i.e., diminish your personal requirements for openings, calls, raises, etc.) when the ante is higher than twice the bet limit; tighten your standards a notch or two when the ante is less than twice the bet limit. The amount of loosening and tightening should, of course, be governed by how much the ante differs from our established norm.

The other factor—tendencies of the players—must also be taken into account. If the game is a loose one and you know from experience that there are often two or more raises before the draw (making the effective bet limit $3 or $4) you must take this into account in computing the ante-bet limit ratio. Loose first-round betting, in effect, raises the limit—act bearish. Similarly, if the game is highly conservative, adjust in the other direction—act bullish. This is another area in which it will be helpful to watch the game you hope to play in for your observation phase. If you have not done your observing as a spectator, you should do it as a participant.

To summarize, adjust your poker style depending on the ratio of the ante to the betting limit—bullish if the ante is relatively high; bearish if the ante is relatively low. If the players in the game have unusual tendencies, take these into account in computing the effective betting limit before comparing with the ante. Once again we see that "rules" must be altered by circumstances if you are to obtain the most effective answers.

POSITION

If I were faced with the casual request, "Teach me something about poker," I would turn to the matter of "position" for my lesson. The reason I expect a lecture on this subject to be effective is not that position is more important than the other poker basics (though its importance is not to be downgraded), nor that I have found, for the first time, a miraculously simple way of explaining a difficult subject, but rather that so few poker players are aware of this factor at all. Or, if they are aware of it, they do not realize how many situations contain positional advantages and disadvantages or how important position can be.

The fact is that position—which means where you are sitting in relation to the order of occurrence of some phase of a poker hand—can be so important that in some forms of poker, position is as important as the cards you hold in your hand!

What is behind this mysterious factor? Let's take a look at it in terms of your poker career. You are at the observation stage and are watching our sample eight-man draw-poker game, sitting behind Bob, who seems to be the big winner in the game. Harry deals—he has dealt so many sample deals in this book that his wrist is probably getting tired—so Al, at Harry's left, is the eldest hand. Al is said to be "under the gun" for reasons which will appear shortly. Anyway, Al opens the betting for the usual $1 and you see that Bob holds:

♠K ♥K ♦J ♥9 ♣2

You, the observer, know by this time that a pair of kings is a moderate hand (as a reader you will not learn this until the next chapter) and you are somewhat surprised to see Bob *drop* with this hand. You make a mental note to ask about this play after the game.

A little later on, Charlie (left of Bob) is dealing. Dick is now under the gun and opens. Ed and Frank drop; George calls; Harry and Al drop, and its Bob's turn. You are astonished to see that his hand is:

♠K ♥K ♦J ♥9 ♣2

You check quickly to make sure that Bob has not forgotten to throw in his cards from several hands ago and are relieved to find that it is only a strange coincidence—the other hand was dealt from the red deck and this one is from the blue deck. Recovering from one shock, you get another when Bob now *calls*. Previously, he had a chance to call with this hand against only one betting opponent, and he dropped. Now, although there are two players in the pot, he decides it is worth a call. What's going on?

The answer is that Bob is *playing position*. In the first instance, his position—his location at the table compared with the order of occurrence of poker events—was very poor. For one thing, there were still six players to speak. If Bob had called and one of the later players had raised, Bob would have been forced to drop—a dollar down the drain. Or suppose one (or two) players had come in after Bob. After the draw, Al (being the opener) would be the first bettor. Bob would be sandwiched between Al, the opener, and unknown quantities behind him. Suppose Al bet after the draw. Bob would have to decide not only if he could beat Al but also what was going to happen with the players who would speak after he did. Or suppose Al checked and one of the players behind Bob had drawn only one card (possibly to a four straight or four flush; we saw on page 61 that with two people already in the pot, it can be good strategy to draw to a four flush). Bob cannot take advantage of the situation even if he has drawn a good hand (such as kings up or three kings). He dares not raise, for the man who drew one card will either drop out (if he missed) or will reraise (if he has made his hand). Either way, Bob can't win any money after the draw and thus loses one of the potential advantages of calling the original bet.

The situation is reversed in the second case. Only Charlie, the dealer, is still to speak after Bob. The chances are that Charlie will drop, but even if he plays, Bob gives away position to one player at most. After the draw, both Dick and George must speak before Bob commits himself. Bob will thus be well placed to determine his action after the draw. The advantage of the second situation over the first was so great, that Bob, *with the identical hand,* dropped in one case and called in the other.

Now you can see why the player to the left of the dealer is called "under the gun." It is the least advantageous place to be, for everyone has a chance to speak after you on the first betting round. (Similarly, the dealer has the greatest positional advantage at the beginning of a deal of draw poker.) Furthermore, when it comes to drawing cards, the man to the left of the dealer must start. Many times it is tremendously advantageous to know how many cards your opponents have drawn. Your own draw may be affected by the knowledge of your opponents' probable hands—you know what you are trying to beat. (More on this in the next chapter.)

Another positional factor of great importance is that the opener automatically puts himself in worst position for the round of betting after the draw, for he must speak first and it is always best to be as close to the end as possible.

Position plays a part of varying importance in every form of poker. For present purposes, it suffices to summarize the three primary positional considerations in draw poker:

(1) The first betting round. The closer to the left of the dealer, the worse the position; the dealer has the best position. It is logical, therefore, that your requirements for opening the pot should be higher when you are close to the dealer's left and lower when you are close to the dealer's right. This will be reflected in later advice.

(2) The draw. The closer to the left of the dealer, the worse the position; the dealer has the best position. This type of positional advantage (or disadvantage) is of importance only when one or more of the players has more than one logical way of drawing to his hand—for either mathematical or deceptive reasons. Of the various positional fac-

tors, therefore, this one is least important, for such hands and situations do not occur often.

(3) The second betting round. The closer to the left of the opener, the worse the position; the opener has the worst position. This form of positional disadvantage is the main reason one must be wary of opening without sound values. By opening, you automatically put yourself in the worst position for betting after the draw.

How much should position affect your play? Very much indeed. When we discuss specific tactics for draw poker, for example, we will see that you should change your requirements for opening considerably depending on your position in the first betting round. Also, the decision of whether to call or raise often depends on what your position will be after the draw—that is, where you will be sitting with regard to the opener (who must bet first after the draw).

Position also plays a part in other forms of poker. While in your observation stage, practice determining the positional value (favorable, neutral, or unfavorable) of each player in each pot. Soon you will be able to evaluate each player's position without conscious thought.

PSYCHOLOGY

Poker psychology deals with what your opponents are thinking. It is profitable to be able to guess what they are thinking and useful to attempt to influence their thoughts.

On the first—determining what your opponent is thinking—I could write much but say little. There are numerous poker situations in which nothing will help you except the ability to decide what your opponent has done. Since I don't know who your opponents will be, I can hardly expect to be able to tell you how they can be expected to behave. But you yourself must be able to decide. How?

The only way to do it—assuming you possess neither clairvoyance nor intuition—is to build up a collection of data on each of your opponents and try to determine his level of skill and his tendencies. This is difficult to manage with a "new" player, one you have never played against before, but should not be too tough when it comes to the "regulars" in your game.

The first thing to determine about each of your opponents is how well he plays. Is he good enough to do this? Does he lack the knowledge to do that? (If you lack any better evidence, you can judge a player's skill by his results.)

Having placed each of your opponents in a skill category, you must keep a record of his tendencies in play. You should observe the values each requires for standard actions. (Some studious players go so far as to make notes after each session.) In attempting this, you can and should make use of the rule that requires each player in a showdown to expose his entire hand.

Clearly, the more experience you have with each opponent, the more you will know about his poker style. When the time comes to make a decision based on psychological considerations, you should be well placed if you have carefully kept track of your opponent's past record. On the other hand, you may be in the dark if you are unfamiliar with his methods.

No more can be said at this stage except that keeping track of your opponents' skills and tendencies is a matter of degree. You may have one game a week to analyze your regular opponents; you may have only one evening to analyze a stranger. Make use of whatever opportunities you have to observe your opponents in action. It is a lazy poker player who does not keep track of what happens on the deals in which he himself does not participate. When you are "out" is the best time to observe how others play.

PAINTING PICTURES

When it comes to painting pictures in the minds of your opponents, I can give more specific advice.

Always attempt to conceal your own style, whatever it is. Remember that your opponents are trying to analyze *your* game as well. Draw attention to plays you have made which are contrary to your usual style.

Why would you play contrary to your usual style? Because if you continually play in the same way, your opponents will eventually get the message. Therefore, keep your style flexible. Or, if there is one style you definitely prefer to all others, turn it on and off according to a predetermined formula.

There is one exception to this: if you are winning, keep doing whatever you are doing, regardless of how obvious your strategy may appear. If it was *that* obvious, you wouldn't be winning! Change horses only if you start losing.

Some players like to conceal their style with a deliberate advertisement at the beginning of a session. The classic case is the solid conservative player who always has the required values and then some when he bets. On the first few deals, he makes a few outrageous bets on weak hands and is soundly defeated. For the rest of the evening, he reverts to his usual style and his opponents continue to call his bets and run up against his supersound values. Well, it sounds nice, but my view is that all this technique will accomplish is to start you off with some losses to make up later on. Except against a completely unsophisticated group, this stratagem is paper-thin. I find it far more effective simply to mix a few nonstandard plays in with the standard ones. Your objective is to keep your opponents guessing and this technique will do it even if they know exactly what you are trying to do.

Superior poker play requires not only that you avoid losing money on your bad hands, but also that you win as much as possible on your good hands. If you bet strongly only when you have a good hand, it will not take your opponents long to mark you as a man not to play against. They will not call your bets and you will find yourself making minimum profits on your good hands and in danger of being eaten into by the antes.

Therefore, you must occasionally bet strongly when you do not have a good hand. This is called bluffing. My main point about bluffing is that you must do it occasionally—it is an important part of keeping your opponents guessing. You may lose on the hands you bluff, but you should get it back when you win more than you are entitled to because your opponents *suspect* a bluff.

But while you must bluff occasionally, don't overdo it. Once in a while is often enough, for a bluff is a risky play and (for most players) loses money on balance—that is, loses more money than it wins in the long run. In order to help dissuade you from bluffing too much, I am going to present only half of the standard advice on bluffing. The standard advice consists of a list of situations in which it is good to bluff and a list of situations in which it is bad to bluff. I will give you only the bad half, for most players will bluff too often and I refuse to do anything which will encourage you down that path to financial loss.

Do *not* bluff: against a weak player; against a big winner;

against a big loser; if you were "caught" in your last bluff and have not won a pot in the interim; if you have not played the *entire* hand exactly as you would have done with a good hand; if you previously bluffed twice (successfully or not) against the same player in this session and were forced to show your cards; if you are losing more than a moderate amount; or, of course, against a player who has a tendency to "keep everyone honest."

If you follow all those rules faithfully, you will not be bluffing too much. In fact, you will be forced to pick your spots for a bluff rather carefully. And that is exactly the attitude you should have toward bluffing.

Above all, remember that a bluff is an attempt to win the pot, *not* an advertisement. The times you are caught bluffing will be publicity enough. Bluff only when you think you have a good chance to get away with it. Don't worry if you are not getting caught in enough bluffs—think of all the hands you are stealing by bluffing successfully. It will be an indication of your improvement as a poker player when you start winning a higher percentage of your bluffs, for it will mean you have become more adept at seizing your opportunities.

The winning poker player does not bluff to lose.

And now, sticking to my word that I have few constructive suggestions to make about psychology at this time— awareness being the most important thing for a beginner or inexperienced player—I bring this lengthy chapter to a close with a suggestion to review it before attempting the quiz that follows. You are not yet ready to sit down at a poker table, but if you can score well on this quiz you may consider that you know quite a bit about poker, and are ready to begin your observation stage (as discussed in Chapter Three).

WIN AT POKER

QUIZ

Each of the questions in this quiz refers to our sample game: draw poker, eight players (in clockwise order: Al, Bob, Charlie, Dick, Ed, Frank, George and Harry), dealer antes $2, betting limits $1 before the draw and $2 after the draw.

1. Harry deals; Al checks; Bob opens for $1; Charlie drops; Dick calls.

    (a) What odds does the pot offer Ed for a call? For a raise?

    Ed raises to $2; Frank drops.

    (b) What odds does the pot offer George for a call? For a raise?

    George calls; Harry and Al drop.

    (c) What odds does the pot offer Bob for a call? For a raise?

    Bob calls; Dick drops.

    (d) How much money is in the pot? What were its sources?

    (e) Who draws cards first?

    (f) List the active players in order of *favorable* position for the drawing of cards.

    (g) Who bets first after the draw?

    (h) List the active players in order of *favorable* position for the betting after the draw.

2. Harry deals; Al and Bob check; Charlie opens for $1; Dick drops; Ed calls; Frank raises to $2; George drops; Harry calls; Al drops; Bob calls; Charlie drops; Ed calls.

    (a) Who draws cards first?

    (b) List the players in order of favorable position for drawing cards.

(c) Who bets first after the draw?

(d) List the players in order of favorable position for the betting after the draw.

3. If you hold:

♠K   ♠Q   ♠J   ♠10   ♦2

and discard the diamond deuce, drawing one card, what are the odds against making:

(a) a royal flush?

(b) a straight flush?

(c) a flush (or better)?

(d) a straight (or better)?

(e) (exactly) a pair of kings?

(f) a pair of kings or better?

(If uncertain about how to do this calculation, compare with the discussion of Harry's hand on page 61.)

SOLUTIONS

1. (a) 4 to 1 on a call; 2 to 1 on a raise.

(b) 3 to 1 on a call; 2 to 1 on a raise.

(c) 8 to 1 on a call; 4 to 1 on a raise. Note that the fact that Bob has already put $1 into the pot has no bearing. That $1 is not forgotten, but it is gone. Bob is now faced with a completely new situation.

(d) Nine dollars: ante $2; Dick $1; Bob, Ed, and George $2 each.

(e) Bob, the first active player to the left of the dealer.

(f) George, Ed, and Bob. George draws last so he is in the best position.

(g) Bob, the opener.

(h) George, Ed, and Bob. George again has the best

position. Positional considerations may have tempted George into calling Ed's raise on the first betting round.

2. (a) Bob, the first active player to the left of the dealer.

(b) Harry, Frank, Ed, Bob. The dealer always has the most favorable position for the first betting round and (if an active player) for the drawing of cards.

(c) Ed. Charlie, the opener, is no longer an active player. Ed is the first active player to the left of Charlie.

(d) Bob, Harry, Frank, Ed. Notice that by checking and later calling, rather than opening, Bob obtained the best position after the draw instead of the worst.

3. (a) 46 to 1. There are 47 possible cards you might draw. Of these, only 1 will give you a royal flush (♠ A); the other 46 will not.

(b) 22½ to 1. This time there are two favorable cards (♠ A, ♠ 9) and only 45 unfavorable cards, so the odds are 45 to 2 or 22½ to 1.

(c) About 4.2 to 1. There are 9 favorable cards (spades) and 38 unfavorable cards, so the odds are 38 to 9 against you.

(d) About 2.1 to 1. In addition to the 9 spades, the other 3 aces and the other 3 nines are now favorable. So there are 15 favorable cards and only 32 unfavorable cards, making the odds 32 to 15, or about 2.1 to 1 against you.

(e) About 14.7 to 1. There are three favorable cards (kings) and 44 unfavorable cards, making the odds about 14.7 to 1 against drawing a pair of kings. This is a pure exercise since no one would mind getting a *better* hand than a pair of kings!

(f) About 1.6 to 1. There are 18 favorable cards and 29 unfavorable cards.

FIVE

◎ ◎ ◎ ◎ ◎

How to Play
Draw Poker

This chapter is designed for your use when you feel ready to advance from the observation stage to your first poker game. (Or, if you are already an experienced player, when you feel you have mastered the principles in the previous chapter.) I have described draw poker in great detail, used it in examples, and now recommend that you begin your poker career with this game. Draw poker has a relatively simple structure. There are only two betting rounds, so strategy can be discussed in a short space, and the basic principles of poker are easily applied to this game—in fact, we have already done so in some of the examples of the previous chapter.

Let's assume that you have found a game that suits you—both temperamentally and financially—have established your limits of loss, have observed for a considerable period of time (preferably this game), and are ready to begin. What tactics should you employ in your efforts to win?

THE FIRST BETTING ROUND

Opening. Position is of paramount importance on the first betting round. It is risky to bet when there are several players yet to be heard from, and by opening the pot you undertake the serious disadvantage of the worst position for the second betting round. Nonetheless, you must open sometimes, lest too many deals be passed out when you have the best hand and you lose a good chance to win the ante. Our first task, therefore, is to establish requirements for opening the pot. These will, of course, depend on your position at the table.

In the chart that follows, I give recommendations for minimum opening requirements depending on your position. Remember that these requirements should be modified if the ratio of ante to opening bet deviates from normal (see "Poker Overhead," page 66). Since this chart refers to the opening bet, it is assumed that all players in front of you have checked.

Opening Requirements (7- or 8-handed game)

Your position	Required to open
Poor (one, two, or three seats left of dealer)	Pair of aces
Average (more or less half-way around the table from the dealer)	Pair of kings
Good (dealer or one or two seats to his right)	Pair of queens or jacks

I recommend that you stick to these minimum requirements. What about the *maximum* hand to open? When should you sandbag (check and hope to raise later) with a very good hand?

In good position, you cannot afford to sandbag for there are few players left to speak and there is a good chance the hand will be passed out. (The most ridiculous example of sandbagging is by the dealer. If he checks, the hand is over!)

With average position, sandbagging seldom pays unless the game is very loose and the players with good position have a tendency to try to steal the ante. Here I recommend an occasional check with a good hand only for the purpose of confusing your opponents as to your style of play.

It is when you have poor position that the check-raise style pays biggest dividends. There are many players yet to speak and the chance of the deal being passed out if you do not open is minimum. Also, by waiting for someone else to open, you can obtain good position for the second betting round and hope to win a big pot. (Reëxamine question 2(d) on page 79 if these positional mechanics are not clear to you.)

As a tactical rule, I recommend checking in poor position on the first round with a hand as good as three of a kind. I add that you must not *always* do this, nor must your check-raise *always* be based on a good hand—just as you should not *always* follow any strategic principle or tactical rule. When you do check a good hand, your plan is to raise if the pot is opened by another player. Do not be too disappointed if you check a good hand and the deal is passed out—you would not have won much by opening anyway.

Calling. Now suppose the pot is opened in front of you. You must decide whether to drop out of the pot or stay in by calling the bet. Positional considerations are still important (be more conservative if sitting near the left of the opener) but an equally crucial factor is how many other players are in the pot. We saw in Chapter Four that a four flush could be a good call or a poor call, depending on how many others were in the pot (for the odds offered by the pot changed). Indeed, when you are considering *drawing* to a good hand—and have no certain values in your hand—the odds almost always should determine your choice of actions. When you are wondering whether or not to call, based on values you already hold, I suggest these guidelines:

(1) If only the opener, or opener and one other player, have entered the pot, *call* with the same values you would have required to open *in opener's position*. (These can be obtained from the chart given above.)

(2) If there are more players in the pot, wait for substantial extra values: a high two pairs if the pot was opened early; a pair of aces if the pot was opened late, or if you will have good position on the second betting round.

Raising. On occasion, you will be faced with the pleasant task of deciding whether or not your values are strong enough for a raise. Once again the number of players in the pot is very important. With only one or two players in the pot, raise with two pairs or better. (However, don't raise with a low two pairs if your position is poor.) Your chance of improving two pairs is not great, and it is generally considered the best strategy to discourage other players from competing. If you permit too many opponents to stay in the pot, one of them figures to improve an original pair and defeat you.* With several players in the pot, do not raise without at least kings up or three of a kind.

Other first-round actions. When it comes to determining whether or not to call another player's raise, and whether or

---

* It should be emphasized that this technique for the play of two pairs is recommended *only* for poker games with limit betting. The considerations are quite different for games with other forms of betting (to be discussed in Chapter Eleven).

not to reraise, the personalities of the players become important factors. Thus, I will not attempt to give a complete list of specific requirements. I think you will find, however, that it pays to be conservative. Tend to believe your opponents at this stage, for there are seldom bluffs before the draw.

For example, if you have opened the pot with what you consider the minimum requirement for your position, and another player has raised, tend to drop out unless the pot offers you unusually good odds for a call. Be conservative also on reraises. Remember that the raising principle applies to reraises as well as raises, and you have no certain knowledge of the strength of the hand of a player who raised. If someone has a **pat hand**—a straight or better, i.e., a hand that can stand pat (draw no cards) on the draw—he could have done no more than raise when it came his turn.

There are percentage standards which can be set down for raises, reraises, etc. The following chart may be used as a rough guide to standards for these actions. (You can make modifications based on the tendencies of players in your game as you gain experience.)

Values for First-Round Draw-Poker Betting

Action	Average expected hand of player taking this action	Values needed to call by player who has not yet bet
First raise	Jacks up (or better)	Aces up
Second raise	Three nines	Three jacks
Third raise	Flush	Ace-high flush
Fourth raise	Jacks full	Queens full
Fifth raise	Aces full	Four of a kind
Sixth raise	Four nines	Four jacks
Later raises	Straight flush	Straight flush

The requirements in the last column apply to a player who must call the full amount of the raise in order to stay in. If you have already put money into the pot, so that you are offered higher odds for a call, you should play on somewhat less. Remember that *if the pot offers good enough odds,* your chance of improvement may justify calling even though you expect to be losing before the draw.

THE DRAW

In the great majority of cases, you will make the draw which is mathematically best for improving your hand: three cards to a pair, two cards to three of a kind, one card to two pairs (or, on rare occasions—when the pot offers good odds—to a four straight, four flush, or four straight flush). There are two reasons why you might deviate from the standard draw: (1) because you wish to confuse the enemy; (2) because you are trying to beat a specific hand.

(1) *Confusion.* You can camouflage your hand in either direction: make believe you have a stronger hand than you have or a weaker hand than you have.

Faking a strong hand is usually part of a bluff. If you haven't been caught in your bluffs very often, a pat-hand bluff may be successful. You bet strongly and draw no cards, making believe you have a straight or better. It is unlikely your opponent(s) have as good a hand, and they will call your bluff bet after the draw only if they suspect you of trickery. If your opponents may suspect you of being "untrustworthy," bluffing three of a kind (by drawing only two cards to a pair) may be more effective, as this is more believable than a pat hand.

Feigning weakness is far more common. Suppose you

have raised with three kings and your raise is called. If you draw only *one* card (which does not cut your chance of improvement very much, by the way), your opponent(s) may place you with two pairs and will thus be tempted to call your bet after the draw if they have a good two pairs or three of a kind themselves.

(2) *Drawing to the situation.* Adjusting your draw to the situation calls for taking advantage of position on the draw. You see how many cards your opponents have drawn and determine your draw by what hand(s) you expect your opponent(s) to have. These draws must be decided on the merits of each case. Here are two of the most common situations which call for an unusual draw because of the action of your opponents:

1. Keeping a high **kicker.** A kicker is an "extra" card held in addition to the basic values in your hand and not exchanged for a new card in the draw. One of the most common errors made by inexperienced draw poker players is keeping a kicker. Thus, with

♥A   ♦Q   ♠Q   ♣10   ♣7

instead of the standard (almost always correct) draw of three cards to the pair of queens, they will keep the ace as well and draw only two cards. Except as a bluff, this is almost always a losing strategy.

Here is one situation in which it *does* pay to keep a kicker. Suppose your hand is:

♠A   ♥A   ♦K   ♦8   ♣2

The pot is opened, one other player calls, and you call. Both of your opponents draw three cards. I suggest you draw only two, keeping the king in addition to the pair of aces. There is a reasonable chance that one of your opponents also has a pair of aces, in which case keeping your kicker will not diminish your chance to improve your hand (unless the other opponent has a pair of kings). If no one else improves—and the odds are that no one will—your kicker may well prove to be the winning difference.

This draw, like all unusual draws, should be attempted only when you feel you can judge your opponent's (or opponents') hands most accurately.

2. Changing your mind. On occasion, you must adjust your draw to meet the needs of the situation. Suppose you hold:

♠A   ♣A   ♠10   ♠8   ♠4

The pot is opened, one other player calls and you call. If both of your opponents draw three cards, you should also draw three cards. You have at least as good a hand as the others going in and your prospects are good.

But suppose one of your opponents stands pat! Unless you suspect a bluff (and possibly even if you do) you should throw away the ace of clubs and try to make a spade flush as your best chance to defeat the opposing pat hand.

The chance of improving. We have seen (pages 60–61) that your decision to stay or drop may depend on the odds offered by the pot and the odds against your winning the hand. The odds against winning the hand often depend on the odds against improving to a specific hand, so it is helpful to memorize a short list of basic odds against improvement. Learn them one or two at a time and the list should fall within a few readings.

Odds against Improving at Draw Poker

Your holding	Number of cards drawn	Hand required	(Approximate) Odds against improvement
One pair	Three	Two pairs (or better)	2.5 to 1
Two pairs	One	Full house	10.8 to 1
Triplets	Two	Full house (or better)	8.7 to 1
Four flush	One	Flush	4.2 to 1
Open-ended four straight (e.g.: 9-8-7-6)	One	Straight	5 to 1

THE SECOND BETTING ROUND

Once the draw has been made and it comes time for betting after the draw, judgment and psychology play paramount roles. You can see your own values; you must form an estimate of each opponent's likely hand based on the number of cards he drew *and his tendencies in drawing.*

Again the keynote is conservatism. Be especially wary of bad position. For example, suppose you opened with a pair of aces and had two callers. All three active players drew three cards and you improved (oh, happy day) to aces up. I recommend a bet, despite your inferior position. It is very unlikely that someone improved enough to beat you and you are likely to get a call "on suspicion," especially if another player made an inferior two pairs.

But now suppose that in the same situation one opponent drew only one card. He probably had a chance to draw a pat hand. If you bet, you are open to a raise. Better to wait and see what action is taken by the player who drew only one card. If he bets, you have a sound call. Thus, you can have a look at his cards without having to pay a reraise. This is a classic strategy often summarized as "never bet into a one-card draw." I don't believe in using "never" when discussing poker, and there are situations in which I would bet even though an opponent drew one card. Nevertheless, if your poker play is sound, you should do well enough without courting unnecessary risks. Thus, especially if you are an inexperienced player or do not have a "book" on the player who drew one card, I do suggest that you *avoid* betting into a one-card draw.

The odds offered by the pot after the draw are of special importance. Sometimes there will have been several calls before the draw, building up a large equity in the pot. Even though the bet limit after the draw is (usually) double what it was before the draw, the pot may offer lucrative odds for a speculative call.

For example, suppose you started with:

♥10   ♦10   ♠8   ♣8   ♣7

The pot was opened and there were two callers before you. You decide to play because you have good position after the draw to look forward to. The other three players draw three cards; you draw one. After the draw, opener bets, the next two players drop. You are very likely beaten since opener bet after the draw despite the fact that you took only one card. But look at the odds. There is now (assuming the stakes of our sample game) a total of $8 in the pot (ante $2; first-round bets $4; opener's bet after the draw $2) and it will cost you $2 to stay in. The pot offers you 4-to-1 odds. While you will probably lose, it is also probably *not* 4-to-1 against you unless opener is an ultra-conservative player. He may have felt you were drawing to a four flush (remember, you would have a good call before the draw with such a hand—see page 61) and tried to use his leverage to get the other two callers out. (By betting in front of the two other callers, opener put them in a difficult position because you drew one card and were sitting behind them with a potential raise.) You should have opener beaten *at least* one time in five, so the odds are less than 4 to 1 against your winning. As the pot offers 4 to 1, I regard this as a sound call.

Finally, beware of making losing calls in the standard "three-man situation." You are in the pot with two others and again are last to speak. The opener bets and the second player calls. Suppose you think either that opener is bluffing or that your values are superior to his. Should you call the bet? Stop! You are thinking about things in the wrong order. What about that "man in the middle"? A man who *calls* isn't bluffing anybody (as opposed to a man who bets first or raises, who might be). Before you think about whether or not you can beat the opener, make sure you have enough to be able to expect to beat the man who called the opener. *He* expects to have a better hand.

JACKPOTS

Your poker group may prefer the jackpots variation in which a pair of jacks is required as the minimum standard to open. What changes should this bring about in your strategy?

The surprising answer is almost none. The only consideration is that you can be assured that opener is not on a complete bluff. This has almost no effect in practical play.

Do not fall into the trap of thinking that the pair of jacks sets up any standards. Stick to the same opening, calling, and raising requirements. Only weak players lower the requirements—by opening whenever they have a pair of jacks or better and by calling with low pairs.

There is one variation of this game which affects certain considerations. Some groups play that when a deal is passed out *another ante is placed in the pot*. This will have the effect of making the ante on the next deal very high compared with the initial bet. When these situations arise, you should become bullish (under the technique outlined on pages 66–69).

Except for this variation, however, play jackpots just as you would ordinary draw poker.

QUIZ

We are finally ready to practice on real-life situations. Again we turn to our sample game. To review the ground rules, the players (in clockwise order) are Al, Bob, Charlie, Dick, Ed, Frank, George, and Harry. The dealer antes $2; betting limits are $1 before the draw and $2 after the draw. The general tenor of the game is conservative.

   1. Al deals; Bob checks.

     (a) Charlie is an aggressive player. What values should he have to open the pot?

     (b) If Charlie opens, what values should Dick have to call?

     (c) Charlie opens and Dick calls. Evaluate the positional advantages and disadvantages of Ed, Al, and Bob at this point.

(d) What odds does the pot offer Ed for a call? For a raise?

2. Bob deals; Charlie opens; Dick, Ed, and Frank drop.

(a) What values should George have to call? To raise?

(b) If George calls, what values should Harry have for a call?

(c) George calls; Harry and Al drop; Bob holds:

♠K   ♥Q   ♦J   ♦10   ♣7.

What should Bob do?

3. Al is very aggressive; Bob—the game's big winner—is ultraconservative. (Yes, this is meant to imply a moral.) Al deals; Bob opens; Charlie and Dick drop; Ed calls; Frank, George, and Harry drop; Al raises; Bob calls.

AL	BOB	CHARLIE	DICK	ED	FRANK	GEORGE	HARRY
...	*Open	*Drop*	*Drop*	Call	*Drop*	*Drop*	*Drop*
Raise	Call			?			

  * Eldest hand

What action should Ed take with each of the following hands:

(a)	♦ J	♠ J	♣ 10	♥ 7	♦ 2
(b)	♦ A	♠ A	♣ 10	♥ 7	♦ 2
(c)	♠ 10	♥ 10	♦ 9	♣ 9	♥ 6

4. Harry deals; Al and Bob check; Charlie opens; Dick calls; Ed, Frank and George drop; Harry calls with:

♠A   ♥A   ♥7   ♥6   ♥3

Al calls; Bob drops. Al draws one card; Charlie and Dick each draw three cards.

AL	BOB	CHARLIE	DICK	ED	FRANK	GEORGE	HARRY
*Check	Check	Open	Call	*Drop*	*Drop*	*Drop*	Call
Call	*Drop*						

. . . .

| | | One | Three | Three | | | |

* Eldest hand

How should Harry draw?

5. Al deals; Bob and Charlie check; Dick opens; Ed and Frank drop; George calls with:

♣K   ♥K   ♦10   ♣6   ♣2

Harry calls; Al, Bob, and Charlie drop. Dick, George, and Harry all draw three cards. George draws ♥8 ♣8 ♠Q, giving him kings up. After the draw, Dick checks.

AL	BOB	CHARLIE	DICK	ED	FRANK	GEORGE	HARRY
. . .	*Check	Check	Open	*Drop*	*Drop*	Call	Call
Drop	*Drop*	*Drop*					

. . . .

| | | | Three | | | Three | Three |

. . . .

| | | | #Check | | | | |

* Eldest hand
# Opening bettor

What action should George take?

6. Harry deals. Al and Bob check; Charlie opens; Dick raises; Ed calls; Frank calls with:

♥Q   ♠Q   ♦Q   ♣6   ♠5

George, Harry, and Al drop; Bob reraises; Charlie drops; Dick calls; Ed drops; Frank calls.

How to Play Draw Poker

Bob and Dick each draw one card; Frank draws two cards to his three queens and gets ♥3 ♥2 for no improvement. After the draw, Dick (the opener) bets.

AL	BOB	CHARLIE	DICK	ED	FRANK	GEORGE	HARRY
*Check	Check	Open	Raise	Call	Call	*Drop*	*Drop*
Drop	Raise	*Drop*	Call	*Drop*	Call		

	One		One		Two		

			#Bet		?		

* Eldest hand
\# Left of seat of opening bettor

What action should Frank take?

SOLUTIONS

1. (a) Under the standards we have established, Charlie should have at least a pair of aces to open in such an unfavorable position. Charlie may be an aggressive player but opening standards should be determined by the nature of the game—in this case, conservative. If Charlie disregards sound standards, he is going to be buried, regardless of his own personal style.

(b) A pair of aces. Here character enters somewhat. If Charlie is so aggressive that he would open with less, Dick may be justified in calling with a little less than usual. (But not too much less, for there are many players yet to be heard from.)

(c) Ed is in pretty good position. It is unlikely that many others will play after him and this will give him good position for the draw and the second betting round. However, this must be modified somewhat because if Ed calls, the pot will offer good odds to a player with, say, a four flush. If someone calls behind Ed and draws one card, Ed's position will be very bad indeed (compare with situation described on page 91).

Al's position occupies a middle ground. If he plays, he must draw cards first, which may put him under some disadvantage. But this is unlikely to be as important as his good position (only Bob has a chance to call behind him) after the draw.

Bob's position is similar to Al's except that he can guarantee himself the best position after the draw since the opener is immediately on his left. This is a good calling position for Bob if he has suitable values.

(d) For a call, 4 to 1; for a raise, 2 to 1.

2. (a) A pair of aces to call, possibly only kings if Charlie is still opening on unsound values. The requirement may be shaded slightly because with several players dropping in front of George, the chance of being hit with a raise is decreased. The pot offers 3 to 1 and that should be enough to play with a hand that will be inferior part of the time but which offers a chance to improve.

In this situation, I would wait for a high two pairs to raise. There is little point to raising with a low two pairs since there will probably be few people in the pot anyway.

(b) Only slightly higher than those for George's call. While Harry has another player to beat, the pot now offers 4 to 1 instead of 3 to 1.

(c) He should drop. The odds against improving to a straight (a probable winning hand) are 5 to 1; the pot offers only 4 to 1. If Harry had called, Bob might consider playing his long shot.

3. (a) Ed should go back to his books. He had no business calling with a pair of jacks in the first place.

(b) I would stick it out, but a drop wouldn't be wrong.

Both Al and Bob may have Ed beaten, but the pot offers 7 to 1 on the dollar Ed must put in to draw cards and it seems just about worth it. This is because Ed has a chance to improve to a hand that will probably win (three aces or possibly aces up). Compare with (c).

(c) Ed should drop. This is a better hand than he had in (b), but his chance to improve is slight and tens up simply are not going to win this hand. Bob, a conservative, opened in an early position and stood a raise. Surely he can beat tens up. Even 8- or 9-to-1 odds from the pot would not justify staying at this point.

4. Three cards to the pair of aces. Al wasn't sandbagging—he didn't raise. Most likely he is drawing to a four flush, tempted by the odds offered by the pot. Neither of the others can have *better* than a pair of aces. Why break up the best hand?

5. He should bet two dollars. After all, he has improved his hand, has no reason to believe anyone else did so, and should therefore make an attempt to win more money in the second betting round. Remember that every so often you will bet as a bluff in situations such as this, so you can expect to get an occasional call "on suspicion" when you have true values.

6. He should drop, and fast. In fact, Frank's call of the reraise before the draw was justified only by his chance of improving.

Three queens is a very good hand, but circumstances alter cases. Bob *reraised* at a time when there were *four* other players in the pot. He knew he would get at least one or two calls—and he sandbagged originally. He simply wasn't kidding! Also, Dick almost certainly has Frank beaten. What is he doing betting into a man who reraised in such unfavorable circumstances?

When this exciting deal occurred, the player I have called

Bob had drawn one card to four sevens! Dick, who had started with three aces (and also made a deceptive draw), had the misfortune to wind up with a full house. Dick's draw was an error, for he was sure to have three of a kind for his strong betting in the first round.

The futility of Frank's calling at this point is demonstrated not only by the actual hands, but by the high probability that Bob will raise again. Frank certainly isn't going to stay for *that* raise—Dick did no more than call it with aces full!—so throwing in two dollars at the point in question is sending good money after bad.

Some of these questions were tricky—deliberately so, for I don't want you to suffer overconfidence. If you had the right ideas on as many as four out of six you are progressing very nicely. A score of two or three right is acceptable, but with a lower score you should go over the last two chapters in a week's time.

Remember that you will gain best advantage from these exercises if you rate yourself honestly.

It's *your* money.

◎ ◎ ◎ ◎ ◎

Stud Poker

Draw poker is called "closed" poker because the hands are kept closed; that is, you don't see any of your opponents' cards until the showdown. This aspect of the game is unappealing or tiresome to some players.

Another aspect of draw poker which some consider a drawback is the limitation to two rounds of betting. Many prefer to be faced with more betting decisions—more opportunities to outwit the enemy.

Still another segment of the poker-playing population dislikes the idea of being forced to pay the considerable ante of draw poker for the privilege of receiving cards. "Why should I have to pay for getting bad cards?" is its war cry.

It was to please pokerites dissatisfied with one or more of these facets of draw poker that stud poker was invented. The main features of stud poker are:

(1) It is "open" poker inasmuch as each player is allowed to see *part* of his opponents' hands. It wouldn't be much fun if one could see *all* the cards, so one or more cards (called **hole cards**) are kept hidden from view. The displayed (open) cards are called **upcards**.

(2) Instead of all the cards being dealt at once (as in draw poker), the players receive upcards one at a time

after obtaining the concealed hole card. There is a betting round after each additional card is received, providing more "action" than draw poker.

It should be pointed out that because of the increased opportunity for betting, the betting limit in stud poker should be lower than in draw poker if the stakes are to be kept comparable. For example, if our typical poker group wished to play stud poker, yet retain the financial "size" of the game, it would probably have a betting limit of a quarter (where it used a dollar in draw poker).

(3) The ante is small; usually each dealer antes an amount equal to the lower betting limit. (Some groups use no ante at all.) In my opinion, such an ante is not intended to play a significant part in the game, but is merely a carryover from the traditions of draw poker.

(4) Stud poker uses different betting rules. In draw poker, there is no way of determining who has the highest-valued poker combination until the showdown. In stud poker, where *part of each hand is exposed,* the players can be ranked after each round is dealt by the portions of the hands which are visible, i.e., the upcards. Within each betting round, the player with the highest *showing* poker combination must act first. In case of (exact) ties, the tied player closest to the dealer's left must act first.

Furthermore, on the first betting round (only), the player designated to speak first is required to open the betting or drop. (After the first betting round, the "high" player may check.) Some poker groups allow a check on the first round (the traditional rule), but I recommend the "bet or drop" rule most highly.

Within each betting round, the betting proceeds as in draw poker, beginning with the designated player. This player may check in any except the first betting round, and should a round be checked out (no one bets), another round of cards is dealt to the active players and a new betting round begins. (Or, if five cards have been dealt, there is a showdown.) It is traditional for the dealer to announce the designated "high" player in order to avoid confusion and accidental bets out of turn. The dealer will say "Pair of sevens bets" or "First ace," meaning the first ace to the dealer's left is designated high, etc.

The betting limit changes in stud poker just as it does in draw poker, but the rules governing the change are somewhat different. Again there are two limits, the second one double the first one. The lower limit is in effect except in two cases: (1) the last betting round; (2) any time a pair (or better) is showing at the beginning of the betting round.*

In a deal of stud poker, each player is dealt one hole card and one upcard to begin. This is followed by a betting round, a second upcard (to the active players), a betting round, a third upcard (to the active players), a betting round, a fourth and final upcard to the active players, a final betting round, and, at last, a showdown. If you have been counting, you will have noted that there are four betting rounds (compared with only two in draw poker), which explains why a poker group will lower the betting limit when switching from draw to stud.

We can now summarize the differences in mechanics between draw poker and stud poker:

* Although few games employ the principle, progressive betting —a boost in the betting limit on each round—can liven up stud poker considerably. I recommend:

First betting round	1 chip
Second betting round	2 chips
Third betting round	4 chips
Final betting round	7 chips

WIN AT POKER

Draw Poker	Stud Poker
All five cards dealt at once; all cards dealt face down.	One hole card and one up-card dealt to begin; other cards dealt face up one at a time.
Right to exchange cards (draw).	No exchange of cards.
Checking permissible.	On the first betting round high man must bet or drop.
Before the draw, player to the left of the dealer bets first; after the draw, opener —or first active player to the left of opener's seat— bets first.	Player with highest *showing* poker combination bets first; ties decided in favor of player closest to dealer's left.
Sizable ante.	Small ante.
Higher betting limit after the draw.	Higher betting limit on the final betting round or when any player has a pair or better *exposed* at the beginning of a betting round. (However, progressive betting is recommended.)
Two betting rounds (one before the draw; one after the draw).	Four betting rounds (one after each upcard is dealt).

Stud Poker

It takes a lot of words to describe these changes, but stud poker is just as easy to understand as draw poker. Furthermore, *it is easier to learn the principles of winning play.* Alas, as we shall see, it is sometimes harder to put these principles into practice than it is draw poker principles.

I began this chapter by listing the reasons some poker players prefer stud to draw. Now that you know what stud poker is, I will tell you some of its drawbacks.

First, since there is no exchange of cards, everyone is stuck with only five cards. Therefore, the hands do not run as high in stud as they do in draw. (The average winning hand in eight-handed stud poker is a pair of kings; in eight-handed draw poker it is jacks up.)

Second, a stud player gets to see five cards only if he sees a hand through to the bitter end. A draw player always sees a full five-card hand.

Which form of poker is better? Don't be silly—it's a matter of individual temperament and personality. Although every poker skill plays a significant part in both games, stud poker emphasizes memory and card analysis; draw poker emphasizes percentages and psychology. Take your choice.

Actually, poker is such a fascinating game that the great majority of players find either form acceptable. I estimate that about half of all players have no preference whatsoever between draw poker and stud poker—they are equally happy with either. This is one of the reasons it is relatively easy to form a poker game; there is usually little bickering about the form of poker to be played.

If you have never played stud poker, give the chart on page 102 a quick rereading. Then we will be ready to discuss stud poker tactics.

WIN AT POKER

HOW TO PLAY STUD POKER

Stud poker holds great temptation for the inexperienced player. The amount he is required to put in the pot seems relatively small; the pot always seems to offer attractive odds. For this reason, almost all errors in stud are errors of overplaying; that is, playing when you should drop. Therefore, I will concentrate on convincing you not to stay as often as you might in the absence of my advice.

First of all, let's explode the fallacy of the pot odds. If there is a small ante, why does the pot usually seem to offer good odds? Answer: In a typical stud game there are a lot of calls on the first round. Why will a lot of people call on the first round? Answer: Primarily because the first bet is almost automatic for the player with the highest exposed card and therefore a signal to start the betting rather than an indication that the opener's hand is strong. (Of course, having the highest card showing, opener's hand is automatically at least relatively good. Also, by having the highest exposed card, he holds the threat of having a card of the same rank in the hole. This is called having a pair back to back. The name derives from the fact that the first upcard is usually placed on top of the hole card, the backs of the cards touching each other.)

Since the ante contributes little to the pot, the pot offers good odds *only when there are a large number of players to defeat.* And that, of course, makes it that much harder to win the pot.

Most stud players tend to throw in their chip—be it penny, nickel, quarter, dollar, or even more—on the first round "to see another card." *This attitude is a sure way to lose.* Actually, proper stud tactics call for exactly the opposite attitude. Because there is only a small ante there is nothing to shoot at. Therefore, profits in stud poker come from winning "developed" pots. Putting it another way, the poker overhead is extremely low. Therefore, for superior stud play, be a bear. (If you don't remember our discussion of bulls and bears at poker, review pages 66–69.)

Now that we have emphasized the essential nature of proper stud strategy—playing it close to the vest—we can proceed to a discussion of specific tactics.

THE FIRST ROUND

Over a period of time, as much money will be won or lost on the first betting round at stud poker as in any other round, even though the lower betting limit is in effect and the amount in the pot is small.

The decision of whether or not to open in the first betting round is similar to that of whether or not to call. So let's consider the two together and discuss the problem of when to call on the first round. Since we are bringing a conservative outlook to stud poker, we will phrase the rules in the negative:

1. *Don't play unless you can "beat the board."* In other words, don't stay in if you cannot make a higher poker combination with your two cards (hole card plus upcard) than any of your opponents can make with only one card.*

2. *Don't play unless you can beat the board.* No, that's not a misprint. It's important enough to be listed twice. Stud poker losses sustained through calling in violation of this rule are *not* tax deductible.

---

* As a matter of poker theory, it is correct to stay without being able to beat the board under certain precise conditions. For example, you should call if you are sure to be no worse than second best, have a good chance to improve, and there are several players in the pot. I recommend that you do not fool around with the exceptional cases until you are an experienced player.

3. *Don't play unless you have one of the following:* a (medium or better) pair, an ace, a king, two cards ten or higher.

4. *Don't play if more than one opponent probably has you beaten.* This is hard to state in precise terms—you must do a little guessing at the probabilities. However, an example of the rule in operation should clarify its meaning. Suppose, in an eight-handed game, you have:

♥5 (upcard)   ♥Q (hole card)

The other upcards are: ♠ 7, ♦ J, ♠ 9, ♥ 6, ♣ 4, ♣ 10, ♦ 10. There are eight aces and kings missing. Except for the man with the four, a player with any of these cards in the hole has you beaten. Furthermore, anyone with a pair or a queen has you beaten. The chances are that more than one opponent has a better hand—so out you go! (Did I hear someone say both cards are hearts? Forget straight and flush possibilities completely.)

5. *Don't play if your cards are matched more than once in the upcards.*

Suppose your hand is:

♥10 (upcard)   ♥K (hole card)

The other upcards are: ♠ 7, ♦ K, ♠ Q, ♥ 6, ♣ 4, ♣ 10, ♦ 10. With all those kings and tens floating around, your chance of improving has been slashed to the bone. Drop at once!

~~em that you will be dropping a high percentage
~~uld and you should. If the thought of
is repulsive to you, and you think
ı enjoyment out of winning money to
ing in as many hands as you might,

then stud poker is not for you. Winning play at stud requires patience, patience, and more patience.

Nor should you worry that your opponents will peg you as a conservative player and that you will not win enough on your good hands to offset your overhead. What overhead? The ante is small, so it costs you little to look at your two cards and throw them away. Your winnings come from the players who cannot bear the thought of not getting into action on enough hands.

Raising on the first round requires special consideration. *As a matter of theory,* you should raise in stud poker whenever you have a hand that outranks those of your opponents. Thus, as we will see shortly, it is normal to raise when you can beat the board and have no reason to believe any other player has a better hand than you do. However, in practice, too many players tend to stay in on the first round of stud poker. Thus, if you are willing to keep a lot of players in the deal, you should avoid raising on the first round for your raise may drive the customers away. Here is a situation calling for this kind of restraint. Suppose you have:

♥K (upcard)   ♦K (hole card)

The other upcards, clockwise from your seat, are: ♥ 6, ♦ Q, ♣ J, ♠ 9, ♦ 10, ♣ A, ♥ 8. The player with the ace bets; the eight is folded (the player holding it drops). Your first impression should be that your hand is "worth" a raise. Indeed, only the player with the ace can have a better hand, and the odds are very high against his having another ace in the hole. Nonetheless, I recommend that you do no more than call. If you raise, most or all of the players behind you will probably drop—you will gain little profit from the deal. But if you merely call, others will call also. You would not mind terribly if anyone raised (with a back-to-back pair)—you would like to see the ace dropped—nor if someone stayed in and paired his upcard on the next round—for you will still have a better hand. Of course, it is *possible* that someone will stay in and later pair an ace in the hole, but if you are going to worry about phantoms like that you should not be playing poker at all. (Another way of looking at this situation is that your position is poor for a raise.)

Contrast this conservatism with my recommendation in the following situation. Here you hold:

♠ J (upcard)   ♣ J (hole card)

The other upcards, clockwise from your seat, are: ♥ 6, ♣ A, ♦ Q, ♣ 9, ♦ 10, ♥ 2, ♥ 8. The player with the ace opens; those with the queen, nine, and ten call; the eight and the deuce are dropped. What's your action?

This time you should *raise!* There is already a bit of money in the pot, and you want to make it as expensive as possible for the other players to stay in and get new cards (which may help them beat your pair of jacks). Even if a higher pair is outstanding, the odds in the pot are high enough to justify calling a reraise. This example is more in line with the guiding principle of betting at stud poker, which we will now discuss.

MAKE IT EXPENSIVE

Let's consider a simplified situation. You are playing stud poker against only one opponent and *all* the cards are dealt face up. An ante equal to the bet limit is paid by each player. Your opponent gets a pair of kings and you receive a pair of aces. You bet, of course. While this bet is obvious, let's examine the basic reason for it: you have the best hand and therefore have a claim to the antes. If you *don't* bet, you give your opponent a *free* chance to improve his hand and take away your equity in the ante money. *Clearly, when you have the best hand, you want to make it as expensive as possible for your opponents to play.* If they call, you have a claim to more money; if they drop, you have deprived them of a chance to "outdraw" you.

Now let's see how to make use of this principle in actual play. Try this situation. You are dealt the dream hand—aces back to back. Your exposed ace is the "high board," and you are forced to bet. A few players call; a few drop. When it comes around to the man on your right, he raises with a king for his upcard. No other aces or kings are showing. The raiser almost certainly has kings (a loose player might have an ace in the hole, but this will worry you even less) and the calls made by the other players correspond to the ante in the simplified example. Should you reraise? No! If you simply call the raise, others will call as well and you will build the pot. If you reraise, everyone else will surely drop out. Your position is bad for a reraise. But suppose the exposed king were on your *left* and the raise was called by several players. What now? Now you should reraise to "make it expensive." By calling you would give everyone a chance to get a better hand at no extra cost.

AFTER THE FIRST ROUND

Here is a guide to winning tactics at stud after the first round. At the outset, I remind you that all your actions must be conditioned by your knowledge of the habits of the other players in the game. The suggestions that follow are recommended for "normal" circumstances and can be used as a base point in your thinking about a decision in stud.

1. If you must have the best hand, or have no reason to believe another player has a better hand, take the lead in the betting, *i.e.*, bet or raise when given the opportunity. (This principle does *not* extend to *reraises*.)

When would you have a reason to believe another player had a better hand? Either because of percentages or the betting by other players. Thus, if you have an eight exposed and a king in the hole, and several other players have queens, jacks, tens, or nines exposed, any of these will have a better hand with an ace, king, or pairing card in the hole. The odds are that one (or more) of them will have such a card, so you have no reason to believe you have the best hand. Do not raise. (Perhaps don't even call!) Or, suppose you have a king exposed and a ten in the hole. You are high and open the betting on the first round. Another player, with an eight exposed, raises. His betting indicates he has an ace or an eight in the hole. You have a reason to believe yours is *not* the best hand. Do not raise back.

2. If you have good values, but have reason to believe yours is not the best hand, do not take the lead in the betting.

In this situation, you must decide not whether to up the stakes, but whether the odds in the pot justify playing at all. Therefore, you will check rather than bet if you have the high board after the first round, and you will not raise.

The only question is whether your hand warrants a call. You should call if:

(1) You can beat the board—but suspect you may not have the best hand *and*

(2) The pot offers no worse than 4-to-1 or 5-to-1 odds on your call *and*

(3) *At most* one of "your cards" (cards of the same rank

as the ones you hold and are therefore trying to match) has appeared on the table.

I mentioned before that it is easy to learn the principles of playing winning stud but hard to apply them. Now we see why: *You must watch the cards to be able to determine your chances.* In fact, the superexpert stud player watches *all* the cards and knows which cards have been folded by players who have dropped from the pot. Until you have gained a great deal of experience, it will be enough for you to watch for the cards you are interested in. Start by counting the cards you are trying to pair. If you start with a king and a queen, watch for cards of those ranks. The next step—all you need attain unless you are interested in the highest levels of play—is to remember also cards which outrank your own (aces in the example above).

How do you learn to count the cards? Just practice, practice, and more practice. A good time to concentrate on counting is during your observation stage, when you need think only about whatever facet of the game you are focusing on, not all of them at once. Get into the habit of remembering critical cards which were folded and it will soon become automatic.

What if you simply can't remember *any* cards, no matter how long and how hard you practice? Then my sincere advice is that stud poker is not for you, except for relaxation at insignificant stakes.

3. If you can't beat the board, *drop.*

Forget the odds offered by the pot; forget which cards have and which have not come out; just *drop.*

I do not intend to go into the details of advanced stud strategy at this point. (I will include a few important situations in the quiz.) However, bear in mind that the basic poker principles presented in Chapter Three apply to stud poker as well as draw.

For example, here is a situation in which *position* plays
an important role. Take Harry's seat in a deal of stud in our
sample game. You are dealt:

♥A (upcard)   ♠J (hole card)

You are high with the ace and bet. Al, on your left, has a
queen and calls; Bob and Charlie drop; Dick calls with a
ten; Ed and Frank drop; George calls with a nine. (All the
players who dropped had small cards.)

On the next round, Al gets a king, Dick an ace, George a
nine, and you a jack, giving you a pair of jacks. The situation now is:

	AL	DICK	GEORGE
Hole card	(?)	(?)	(?)
First upcard	♥ Q	♠ 10	♦ 9
Second upcard	♦ K	♠ A	♣ 9

	YOU	
Hole card	(♠ J)	Pot: $1.25
First upcard	♥ A	
Second upcard	♦ J	

There is $1.25 in the pot (quarter ante plus four quarter
bets on the first round). George has a pair of nines so that
the betting limit moves up to the high limit—fifty cents.
George bets. What should you do?

Answer: Drop! You have a good hand, but your position is
terrible. Al threatens you with a pair of kings or queens;
Dick played with a ten on the first round and may have an
ace in the hole. Perhaps you have the best hand at this stage
(the probability depends on the styles of the players in-

volved) but there is a good chance of a raise behind you, so you have too little to win and too much to lose by playing. Your position is terrible. Notice that stud position depends on where you sit in relation to the man with the high board.

Suppose the situation were mirrored, as follows:

	GEORGE	DICK	AL
Hole card	(?)	(?)	(?)
First upcard	♦ 9	♠ 10	♥ Q
Second upcard	♣ 9	♠ A	♦ K

	YOU
Hole card	(♠ J)
First upcard	♥ A
Second upcard	♦ J

George bets fifty cents and the others call. You are in good position and I recommend that you call. The pot offers over 5-to-1 odds and you will very likely get a chance to see the action before deciding your bet on the next round. (Normally, George will remain high.) Since you cannot get sandwiched between an opening bet and a potential raiser, your chance of being high plus your chance of improving certainly justify a call at 5-to-1 odds.

Although this chapter has covered only about half of the sort of decisions you will be faced with in a stud game, the others depend to a great degree on your experience with the players involved. If you have taken in all the preceding, you will be off to a flying start toward effective stud play.

Try your hand at the quiz, bearing in mind that a few new twists are introduced.

Oh yes, a final bit of advice on stud. Your hole card is for you alone to see. If you keep peeking at it to make sure it is still there, you increase the chance someone else will catch a glance of it. Look at your hole card when you get it. *Memorize it.*

Never look twice at your hole card.

QUIZ

All situations in this quiz refer to our typical game. When playing stud poker, Al, Bob, Charlie, Dick, Ed, Frank, George, and Harry (sitting clockwise around the table) use a twenty-five cents ante by dealer, a twenty-five cents betting limit with no pair showing before the last round, fifty-cents limit with a pair showing and on the last round.

1. The upcards seen by Harry, starting at his left, are:

AL	BOB	CHARLIE	DICK	ED	FRANK	GEORGE
♥8	♦Q	♠A	♥10	♠8	♣J	♣K

Charlie bets; Dick and Ed drop; Frank and George call. What should Harry do with each of the following hands:

(a)	Upcard:	♠ 3;	Hole card:	♠ 4
(b)	Upcard:	♠ 3;	Hole card:	♥ K
(c)	Upcard:	♥ Q;	Hole card:	♦ K
(d)	Upcard:	♦ 8;	Hole card:	♦ A
(e)	Upcard:	♥ J;	Hole card:	♦ A
(f)	Upcard:	♥ 3;	Hole card:	♠ 3
(g)	Upcard:	♥ J;	Hole card:	♦ J
(h)	Upcard:	♣ A;	Hole card:	♠ 2
(i)	Upcard:	♣ A;	Hole card:	♦ 7
(j)	Upcard:	♣ A;	Hole card:	♦ 8

(k) Upcard: ♣ A; Hole card: ♠ K
(1) Upcard: ♣ A; Hole card: ♥ A

2. With the same upcards, Charlie opens; Dick and Ed drop; Frank calls; George raises. What should Harry do with each of the following hands?

(a) Upcard: ♥ Q Hole card: ♥ A
(b) Upcard: ♣ A Hole card: ♥ Q
(c) Upcard: ♣ A Hole card: ♥ A

3. Harry holds: Upcard: ♦ K   Hole card: ♠ A
High on the first round, Harry bets; Bob, Dick and Frank call, the others folding two fives, a six, and a four. After the next round of cards, the situation as Harry sees it is:

	BOB	DICK	FRANK
Hole card	(?)	(?)	(?)
First upcard	♠ Q	♦ 8	♣ J
Second upcard	♥ 10	♣ 6	♠ K

	HARRY	
Hole card	(♠ A)	
First upcard	♦ K	Pot: $1.25
Second upcard	♥ 9	

(a) Frank (now high) checks. What should Harry do?
(b) What should Harry do if Frank bets?
(c) If Frank's second upcard had been the ♣ 4, leaving Harry high, what should Harry do as first to speak?

4. Harry holds: Upcard: ♥ Q   Hole card: ♠ A

The other upcards are:

AL	BOB	CHARLIE	DICK	ED	FRANK	GEORGE
♠2	♦K	♦5	♠J	♦10	♠8	♥K

Harry was the dealer, so Bob has the first king to the left of the dealer. Bob bets; Charlie drops; Dick calls; Ed drops; Frank and George call; What should Harry do?

5. In question 4, right or wrong, Harry calls. Al drops. After the next round of upcards, the situation is:

	BOB	DICK	FRANK	GEORGE
Hole card	(?)	(?)	(?)	(?)
First upcard	♦ K	♠ J	♠ 8	♥ K
Second upcard	♣ 2	♦ 3	♠ 7	♣ 10

Pot: $1.50

	HARRY
Hole card	(♠ A)
First upcard	♥ Q
Second upcard	♠ 6

George checks. What action should Harry take?

6. In question 5, Harry, Bob and Dick check. Frank bets; George calls. What should Harry do now?

7. In question 6, Harry calls; Bob drops; Dick calls. After the next round of cards, the situation is:

DICK	FRANK	GEORGE
(?)	(?)	(?)
♠ J	♠ 8	♥ K
♦ 3	♠ 7	♣ 10
♥ 3	♥ 2	♦ A

Stud Poker

Pot: $2.50   HARRY

　　　　　(♠ A)
　　　　　♥ Q
　　　　　♠ 6
　　　　　♥ A

Dick, high on board with a pair of threes, checks; Frank checks; George bets (fifty cents, since a pair is showing). What action should Harry take?

8. In question 7, Harry calls. Dick and Frank drop. The last card is dealt and the situation is:

	GEORGE	HARRY
Pot: $3.50	(?)	(♠ A)
	♥ K	♥ Q
	♣ 10	♠ 6
	♦ A	♥ A
	♦ Q	♣ 3

George bets (fifty cents, it being the last betting round). How do you "read" the hands of the players who were active in this deal? What should Harry do?

SOLUTIONS

1. (a), (b), (c). Drop in each case. You can't beat the board. Hand (c) is a potential exception to the beat-the-board rule, but both of your cards are matched in the up-cards, cutting your chance of improving.

(d) Drop. You may have the best hand, or almost the best hand, but there are two eights showing and your chance of improvement is slight. You have no overhead to worry about, so fight on a less rainy day.

(e) Call. There is a fair chance you have the best hand.

(f) Drop. With so many higher upcards, you have little chance of remaining high. The pot odds (4 to 1) are not high enough.

(g) Raise. With another jack showing, and considering the size of the other upcards, this hand is little better than a pair of threes. You want people out, not in.

(h) Drop. Charlie at least must have you beaten; possibly others do as well. The pot odds aren't high enough to warrant a speculation. It is a disadvantage to have a weak hole card, for you cannot profit from the element of surprise.

(i) A marginal situation. You have more or less half a chance of having Charlie beaten. I would drop because of the indifferent hole card.

(j) Drop. Except for advertising value, this hand is no better than the one in (d).

(k) Raise. This is sort of daring, but you don't want to raise *only* when you have a back-to-back pair—no one will ever call you—when you have the high upcard. You are somewhat protected here by the fact that you may well have the best hand anyway.

(l) Raise, unless your last few raises in this situation have been with a "sure best" hand. Anyway, do the same thing frequently on (k) and (l) to keep them guessing. If you are known as a conservative, just call and hope to build a big pot for later picking.

2. (a) I would drop. George's possibilities are limited: he has an ace, a king, or a bluff. If he has an ace or a king,

he has a strong advantage over you—the more so as two of
"your cards" are showing on board. Even if George is
bluffing, your chance of improvement is not so great that
you want to take a chance with only 2½-to-1 odds in the pot.
After all, what are you going to do next round if you have
not improved and George bets again?

(b) Drop, surely. Compare with (a). This time George
bet with two aces exposed on the table. The chance that he
is bluffing is way down, and it is not even too likely he has
an ace in the hole.

(c) Call—don't raise. There are three reasons for not
raising at this point: (1) you want to lure others into the
pot if possible; (2) in particular, you want to give Charlie
every inducement to stay in—by keeping him in action, you
may get into good position *behind* George (if Charlie gets
the high board); (3) you want to misrepresent your hand
in case you wind up against George, or—a long shot—if
Charlie also has a pair of aces.

Notice that by merely calling George's bet, you almost
insure that Charlie will stay in. He has an ace, and the pot
will offer him at least 7 to 1 to stay in, since he need pay
only twenty-five cents to play. But if you raise, he will have
only about 4-to-1 odds from the pot and will have an extra
potential strong man to consider.

Remember that very strong hands must sometimes be
treated with tender loving care.

3. (a) Check, unless Frank is a weak player. Otherwise,
whatever Frank started with, the king has given him a very
strong hand and he must be sandbagging. Always "respect"
the player who drew a (potentially) good card.

(b) Call. Frank had only George to "keep in" by not
raising with jacks on the first round, so he probably hasn't
got them. He may have made a pair of kings, but more

likely he just thinks he has the best (or near-best) hand. The pot offers 6-to-1 odds and this is too good an opportunity to pass up. Dick's possible pair of eights should not frighten you, since Dick is unlikely to raise back into Frank's potential reraise with kings.

(c) Bet. The fact that Frank's hand is worse doesn't make Harry's any worse. Even if Dick has a pair of eights, Harry has three ways to draw a superior hand.

4. Harry should call. There is no question of dropping out with an ace and two high-ranking "live" cards. But there is little to be gained by raising, for to do so would shorten the odds. Harry's hand is simply not strong enough to raise. (Compare with discussion of hands worth calls but not raises, page 66.)

5. Check. The main danger at this point is that Frank has a pair of eights. Since the six, although a "live" card, will not beat eights if paired, Harry doesn't want to start upping the stakes in case Frank decides to start betting. Also, a check at this point will give Harry some information about the strength of Bob's hand. Bob was forced to open on the first round and is an unknown quantity.

6. A close question. I might drop out if suspicious of George. But I'm very conservative and the pot does offer Harry 8-to-1 odds at this point—not bad considering his queen is still "live" and his ace may be as well.

Another reason for Harry calling is that if he dropped out I would have to think up a new example hand, whereas this way I can squeeze another few questions into the same setup.

7. Here conflicting factors enter. If Harry were battling solely against George (who presumably has an ace in the hole), he would certainly have a call. No queens or sixes have shown, so just the chance of Harry "hitting" a queen or

Stud Poker

six is enough to justify his playing against George, for the pot offers greater than 5-to-1 odds.*

Also, George may not have what he advertises. But there is Dick to consider. He may well have been lying back earlier, and now have something. So a call by Harry involves some risk. Dick may well be about to raise.

But even so, Harry cannot have *much* the worst of it, and his fears from both George and Dick may be unfounded. Hard as it is to give up a good hand, one must do so when the odds become highly unfavorable. It looks as if George has a pair of aces, so Dick may have two pairs.

Nonetheless, it is also a poor policy to be pushed out of the pot too easily when you have sound values. Suppose Dick *does* raise, and it costs Harry an additional fifty cents beyond the present fifty-cents call to stay in to try to draw a queen or a six. Harry will still be getting about 4 to 1 on his money—and the odds against his drawing are only a little higher than 4 to 1. The potential disadvantage of Dick also improving counts against Harry, but it doesn't amount to much.

So in the end, Harry should call. The following principle applies in the case at hand:

---

* The computation of the chance that Harry will draw a queen or a six for his last card is fairly complicated. I include it here not so much because it is basic but because it will probably be of interest to you after you have become adept at counting cards—sometime in the future.

Harry has seen 18 cards thus far (4 of his own, 3 each "on board" for Dick, Frank and George, 2 for Bob, 1 each for Al, Charlie, and Ed) and presumably neither Dick nor Frank nor George has a queen or six in the hole. So 21 cards are accounted for, leaving 31 unknown. There are 6 queens and sixes unseen, so the odds are therefore 25 to 6—slightly above 4 to 1—against Harry drawing a queen or a six. Thus, 5-to-1 pot odds would justify a call, since aces up will almost surely give Harry the pot.

It is worth making a *slightly* disadvantageous bet to guard against the possibility that you have misread the opponents' hands.

Since Harry is the hero on the white horse, Dick drops out (as does Frank). So Harry has made a good call, even if George has the "case" ace in the hole. (The case card of a rank is the last missing card. Harry sees three aces, so George will have the last possible ace if he has one in the hole.)

However, as we will see in the next question, Dick's drop has a great deal of significance.

8. Believe it or not, Harry should *raise!* To see how Harry should reach this conclusion, let's analyze the hands of the other players. Frank's hand is not hard to determine. He started with a pair of eights, opted not to raise on the first betting round, tried to get people out (or make it expensive for them to draw against him) on the second betting round, and folded his tents when it became apparent there was bigger stuff out against him.

Now what about Dick? Surely he hasn't a three or a jack in the hole, for he would hardly drop an immortal on the third betting round. So what is his hole card? How about an ace or a king? Would Dick play originally and call Frank's bet with a king in the hole? With two other kings showing at the beginning, Dick would hardly play this way unless he is an *extremely* loose player—but he can't be that loose, for he folded the high board on the third round, and very loose players certainly don't do that. So Dick had an ace in the hole and made a slightly aggressive call of Frank's bet (but remember that no aces or jacks were showing at that time). The rest of his plays are now easy to understand.

But if Dick had an ace in the hole, then George didn't. Three aces are visible to Harry and there are (presumably) only four in the deck! If George doesn't have an ace in the hole (what a surprise!), he can beat Harry only if he started with a jack in the hole—no doubt you noticed that straight possibility.

If George's hole card is a jack, Harry should pay off. For George's entire series of plays does not make sense if his hole card is a jack. Why call Frank's bet with K-J-10? (Three of his cards were out—Ed folded a ten—and Harry, Bob and Dick were all unknown quantities sitting behind him.) On drawing the ace, why bet and increase the stake on the chance of filling in a queen? (There was a fairly good chance Dick was lying in the bushes, or that Harry had a pair of aces or queens. Would not George have been delighted to have a *free* chance to try to hit a queen?)

So what is George doing? If he can't have an ace or a jack in the hole, the only card that makes sense is a king. And now we can uncover George's clever manipulations on this deal—which, by the way, are going to cost him heavily. He started with a pair of kings when no aces were on board and (quite reasonably) set out to win a big pot. He called on the first round to give room to Harry and Al to enter the pot cheaply. Upon getting the high board, he checked, presumably in deference to Frank's potential pair of eights. When he then called Frank's bet, he gave the impression of a man with an ace in the hole who was going out to beat the eights. Thus, from his point of view, others with high cards followed suit, being offered good odds from the pot.

The exposed ace of diamonds spoiled George's representation of weakness—since he had been making believe all along that he had an ace in the hole. So he had to change horses in midstream. Recognizing the possibility that Harry had an ace in the hole, he stayed true to his bluff and bet into the teeth of a potential two pairs in Dick's hand, now trying to get Harry out by forcing him to commit himself before Dick was heard from.

On the final round, George saw he could beat Harry unless Harry had an ace in the hole, so he continued his make-believe pair of aces (king next!) in the hope of convincing Harry that opposition was hopeless. (The straight possibility was just window dressing for the example.)

Where George's "luck" ran afoul was when Harry was able to read Dick's hole card accurately.

This example is based on an actual deal in an expert poker game. When "Harry" raised on the last round, "George" eventually decided Harry had started with a pair of queens and thinking himself beaten, was making a last-ditch effort to indicate that he had discovered George's phony representation of his hand and was playing him for (perhaps) a pair of tens.

So George called with his pair of kings and Harry won a big pot. (The stakes were "slightly" higher than twenty-five cents and fifty cents.)

RATING YOUR GAME

If you stayed with the analysis of the final deal as far as halfway, you have probably mastered most of the material in this chapter. If you were thinking along the right lines in questions seven and eight, your performance is superlative. (If you got them right through question eight, stay away from my game. I need the money.)

The analysis of the final hand shows that it is not enough merely to consider the possible hands of the active participants. Your assessment of the possibilities must include as many of the facts as you can marshal. Harry could hardly have come to the winning conclusion at the end if he had disregarded Dick just because that player was no longer active. While I admit that this spectacular analysis was on a high level—and one that only an expert would reach—this is the *type* of thinking that leads to success at stud poker.

I'll have a bit more to say on this in the chapter on "Improving Your Play" (see Chapter Eleven).

SEVEN

◎ ◎ ◎ ◎ ◎

Opportunity Knocks?

You may have judged from the amount of detail in the previous chapters that I consider standard five-card draw and stud the safest games for the inexperienced player who wishes to get his feet wet in the ocean of poker variations. And I do, for these games add little more than a few special situations to the list of musts for successful play at all games.

In this chapter, we move into the danger zone; the variations described henceforth are not so safe. The knock on your door may be the bill collector rather than opportunity. In order to prevent you from leaping before looking, I will restrict the discussion somewhat and add a warning that you will need more than the advice in this book to play these games well.

We have seen that the primary disadvantage of draw poker is the restriction to two rounds of betting whereas the main drawback of stud poker is the lack of good poker hands. Is there a happy medium which avoids both difficulties? The most satisfactory solution thus far achieved is one which transcends one of the most time-honored traditions of poker—that poker is a game played with five cards. Modern variations of poker are games played with *more than five cards dealt to each player.* There is no change in the nature of poker hands—five cards are still used in determining the value of each player's hand. However, one may receive six or seven (or even more) cards *from which to select his best poker hand of five cards.*

As extra cards plus a draw would make it too easy to get a good hand, extra-card games are usually restricted to stud poker. Furthermore, the majority of players have found that **seven-card stud** is the most interesting among games with more than five cards. In fact, in recent decades seven-card stud has been gaining popularity faster than any other form of poker.

RULES OF SEVEN-CARD STUD

Except for the mechanics of dealing the cards and the specification that each player in the showdown may select any five of his cards to form the best possible poker hand, seven-card stud is no different from five-card stud. Therefore, the only topic requiring discussion is the method of dealing the cards.

As you will recall (Chapter Five), five-card stud begins with each player being dealt *one* hole card and one upcard; in seven-card stud, a deal begins with each player receiving *two* hole cards and one upcard. Five-card stud continues with three more rounds of upcards; seven-card stud does likewise. At this point, five-card stud is ready for a showdown—each player has five cards. However, only six (of seven) cards have been dealt for the seven-card game, so seven-card stud concludes with the final card dealt *face down* (giving each still-active player three hole cards and four upcards), followed by a final betting round and then the showdown. There is only one additional betting round in the seven-card game, for although there are two extra cards dealt, one of these (the second original hole card) does not necessitate a betting round. It may be convenient to compare the two games through the following chart.

Comparison of Five-Card and Seven-Card Stud
(differences italicized)

Five-card Stud		Seven-card stud
One hole card	(Dealt)	*Two hole cards*
One upcard	originally	One upcard
	FIRST BETTING ROUND	
Second upcard		Second upcard
	SECOND BETTING ROUND	
Third upcard		Third upcard
	THIRD BETTING ROUND	
Fourth upcard		Fourth upcard
	FOURTH BETTING ROUND	
		Final hole card dealt
		Fifth Betting Round
Showdown		Showdown

As in five-card stud, seven-card stud uses a small ante and a "bet or drop" rule for the high man on the first round, and has a higher betting limit on the last betting round, or when any player has a pair or better among his upcards.

HOW TO PLAY SEVEN-CARD STUD

The basic tenets of good poker play (Chapter Four) and of winning stud strategy (Chapter Six) carry over into seven-card stud. If you are not thoroughly familiar with these, you should proceed no further in this chapter until you have mastered them. Don't be ashamed to review preliminary material before attempting what is built upon it. You should not continue with this section without a firm understanding of what has preceded, nor should you play seven-card stud until you can play five-card stud with confidence. I know it sounds repetitious, but this cannot be overemphasized.

Despite all the poker knowledge that you can bring to seven-card stud based on your sound technique at five-card stud, the fact that more cards are (potentially) involved means that you will have to readjust your hand valuation.

In seven-card stud three eights or three nines is the average winning hand. In five-card stud, the average winning hand is a pair of kings or aces. Notice the enormous difference between the average winning hands in five-card and seven-card stud. Those two extra cards really change things.

THE FALLACY OF TRYING TO IMPROVE

The most important pitfall to avoid when playing seven-card stud is counting too heavily on possible straights and flushes. Suppose, for example, that in your first five cards you have four to a flush. Since you are entitled to *two* more cards, the chance of your filling the flush is reasonably good, and the pot may offer tempting odds. The fly in the ointment is that if your sixth card does not fill the flush, the odds against making it on the last card will rise enormously. Since the pot odds will not keep up with the odds against making your flush (especially as there will usually be an open pair by that time and the bet limit will increase), *you will not be able to see the hand through to the end.* This must be taken into consideration when you consider calling after the *fifth* card.

Furthermore, a straight, flush, or low full house does not have anywhere near the security it does in draw poker. When we discussed drawing to a straight or flush in draw poker, we were justified in making the simplifying assumption that if you made your hand you would win the pot. But in seven-card stud, where the hands run so much higher, *this is not a proper assumption.* The effect of making your straight or flush may be that you lose even more money when you are raised at the end and run into a full house.

Therefore, I recommend that you forget about straight and flush possibilities *unless they are based on high-ranking cards which can be turned into pairs and triplets.* Throw away hands which offer no more promise than a straight or flush possibility and you will be a big winner in the long run.

What you *should* try for is a high three of a kind (which can be turned into a *high* full house if improved). So the best thing to start with is a high pair. But *not* a low pair, for the addition of a second low pair will *not* give you a suitable hand for continuing play. Based on this discussion, we can formulate the requirements for playing at the beginning of a hand of seven-card stud.

Basic requirements (in first three cards) *for staying in* (i.e., calling) *a deal of seven-card stud:* a high pair (jacks or better); a medium pair *with the entire pair concealed* (for surprise value) and a high upcard; three high cards which offer both pairing *and* straight or flush possibilities (Q-J-10 or better, or three to a flush including three high cards or an ace and one other high card). Your cards offer pairing possibilities if they are unmatched among the other upcards. The most important consideration on the first betting round is: *do not stay in with a small pair.*

Raising on the first round (uncommon when there are so

many betting rounds) is largely a matter of whether you want people in or out, and do or do not want to take the lead in the betting. The best time to raise is when you are in good position and have *concealed* values, such as a high pair in the hole.

THE ADVANTAGE OF CONCEALMENT

In the requirements for staying in a pot of seven-card stud on the first round, I accept a weaker poker combination *if the value of the hand is concealed.* For example, under normal circumstances, I would play with a pair of queens however they were dealt (**concealed**—both in the hole—or **split**—one in the hole and one face up). However, with a pair of *tens,* I would stay only if the entire pair was concealed (and my upcard was jack or higher).

The reason one can afford to play on lower values when they are concealed is the advantage of surprise. If you have a split pair and are lucky enough to be dealt a third card of the same rank, giving you triplets, all the other players will know you have improved your hand. However, if you match your concealed pair, your helpful card will be just another upcard from the point of view of your opponents. Contrast these situations:

1. Split pair improved		2. Concealed pair improved
(♠ J)	Hole	(♠ J)
(♣ Q)	cards	(♥ J)
♥ J	Upcards	♣ Q
♥ 9		♥ 9
♦ J		♦ J

You stayed after drawing the heart nine because you retained some chance for a straight along with your high pair. After the fifth card (♦ J), the player in number 1 has upcards which seem powerful. He cannot conceal his true strength. The player in number 2, however, seems to have no more than a possible straight. If several tens have shown, no one will pay much attention to him. Yet, he is lurking with three jacks and may win a big pot if he completes a full house while another player makes a flush (and interprets the strong betting of player 2 to indicate a straight).

Notice that because of the large number of hole cards, it is possible to make a full house *without ever showing a pair in the upcards*. For example, player 2's final hand might be:

Hole	(♠	J)
cards	(♥	J)
	(♦	9)
Upcards	♣	Q
	♥	9
	♦	J
	♠	6

It doesn't look as if he has much if you look only at what he is showing. This strategy cannot be applied often in five-card stud, for you have only one concealed card and the possibilities are limited. In seven-card stud, one must be wary of "icebergs"—hands which have most of the values concealed.

Since it is this surprise element which leads to the winning of the largest pots, the requirements for playing in the early rounds may be reduced when you retain the possibility of keeping your values concealed, thus lulling your opponents into a false sense of security.

LATER TACTICS

The fourth card is crucial. Once again, you should follow a rule which will lead to conservative play. *If your fourth card does not improve your hand, drop unless your original values were outstanding (e.g.: a pair of aces).* If you had a minimum "stay" on the first round, the very least you should require from your fourth card is that it give you another pairing possibility (i.e., is unmatched among the other upcards). Remember that if you are dealt a useless card for your second upcard, you are competing with only three cards while others have four. True, some of your opponents also will have received no further help. But you cannot count on *all* of your opponents remaining with their original values. Staying in with a useless card (on the early rounds) is equivalent to a major-league pitcher never throwing his fast ball. In extreme cases, it can be as serious a disadvantage as boxing with one hand tied behind your back.

Thus, if you started with a pair, you should drop after the fourth card unless you now have triplets, two pairs, or an additional *high* card which offers good pairing possibilities. If you started with a straight or flush possibility, drop after the next card unless it strengthens that hope (or, in some cases, if you now have a high pair). If you started with anything less, go back and reread the beginning of this chapter.

BLUFFING AT SEVEN-CARD STUD

A surprisingly large number of players find bluffing more attractive at seven-card stud than at five-card stud. They, in turn, are surprised at how infrequently their bluffs succeed. There is a good reason for this, in fact, two good reasons.

1. A bluff is less likely to succeed at seven-card stud (than five-card stud) because the odds offered by the pot at the point of the bluff are generally greater. Remember that seven-card stud has an extra betting round, another opportunity for the pot to build up. Further, inexperienced players tend to play more loosely than they should in the early rounds because there are so many more cards to come. They might miss out on something if they dropped early. Therefore, seven-card stud pots tend to be much larger than five-card stud pots. Accordingly, it is more tempting to call a bet at the end because the pot offers such good odds that it is worthwhile taking out insurance against a possible bluff. It therefore follows that few bluffs succeed at seven-card stud.

2. As if this weren't enough, it is almost impossible to gauge a situation precisely enough to know when a potential bluff has a good chance to succeed. This is because of the large number of concealed hole cards held by each player. On occasion, in five-card stud, you will be tempted to bluff with a weak hand because you feel your opponent also holds a weak hand (though a little better than yours) and will not be able to call a bet. But when your opponent has *three* concealed cards, how can you judge accurately when this situation has arisen? In fact, as we have seen, your thinking should be quite the reverse. Instead of thinking how *weak* your opponent might be, think about how *strong* he might be.

Because late-round bluffs are so unlikely to succeed, even in apparently favorable situations, one should avoid betting a hand of seven-card stud with the aim of an eventual bluff. It just won't work.

The rest of my advice on seven-card stud is also directed towards conservatism. The most important feature of playing seven-card stud is getting out fast—at least, as fast as possible. Therefore, you should drop (*not* see "just one more card") if:

(1) more than one card matching the ranks you are hoping to pair appears in the other upcards;

(2) any opponent gets an open pair and you have no higher-ranking pair;

(3) you cannot beat each of your opponents on the assumption that each has one perfect hole card and one useless hole card.

In short, don't get involved in a hand of seven-card stud without sound values. With *three* hole cards (eventually), your opponents might turn up with almost anything. Beware—this is *not* a game which rewards playing on possibilities.

SIX-CARD GAMES

You are not likely to run into a group which prefers six-card stud, but it won't hurt to become familiar with the mechanics just in case. Six-card stud begins like five-card stud, with one hole card and one upcard, and continues in the same manner through three more upcards. When it would be time for a showdown in five-card stud, a second hole card (sixth and final card) is dealt, followed by a betting round and a showdown.

You should play this game very much like five-card stud insofar as first-round tactics and basic overall strategy are concerned. Keep the same requirements for calling and raising in the early rounds. With only six cards, straights and flushes do not play a big part in the game. The average winning hand (in an eight-handed game) is tens-up.

Above all be conservative—if you aren't sure whether to stay in or not, *don't*.

A final piece of information about six-card stud: if you run into a poker group which deals the *fifth* card down and the sixth card up (reversing the normal procedure), do some extra watching before playing. This variation is typical of expert poker games. (You might remember this if your game feels in need of a status symbol.)

QUIZ

In this quiz you are engaged in seven-card stud. Our usual stud rules apply: eight players; dealer antes twenty-five cents; betting limit twenty-five cents until a pair shows or before the last round; betting limit fifty cents when a pair shows and on the last betting round.

1. On the first betting round, you are faced with the following array of opponents' upcards, clockwise from your left:

♥ 8   ♦ K   ♥ J   ♣ 10   ♦ J   ♣ A   ♠ 6

The player with the ace, holding the high board, bets; the player with the six drops.

What action do you take with each of the following hands?

	Hole cards		Upcard
(a)	♣ 9	♦ 7	♣ 6
(b)	♥ 7	♥ 5	♥ 2
(c)	♠ A	♦ 7	♣ 6
(d)	♠ A	♥ K	♠ J
(e)	♥ 7	♦ 3	♦ 7
(f)	♠ J	♣ J	♥ 10
(g)	♠ Q	♥ 5	♦ Q
(h)	♠ Q	♦ Q	♥ 5
(i)	♣ 3	♦ 3	♥ 3
(j)	♥ A	♠ A	♠ Q

Opportunity Knocks?

2. You are sitting behind Harry in our sample game, and he deals as follows: (Players listed clockwise from Harry's left.)

	AL	BOB	CHARLIE	DICK	ED	FRANK	GEORGE
Hole	(?)	(?)	(?)	(?)	(?)	(?)	(?)
cards	(?)	(?)	(?)	(?)	(?)	(?)	(?)
Upcard	♥ 2	♠ A	♣ 3	♦ K	♦ 10	♦ 8	♠ 2

	HARRY	
Hole cards	(♠ J)	(♥ J)
Upcard	♠ 10	

Bob, with the ace, bets; Charlie drops; Dick calls; Ed drops; Frank calls; George drops. What should Harry do?

3. In Question 2, Harry calls; Al drops. After the next round of upcards, the situation is:

	BOB	DICK	FRANK	
Hole cards	(?) (?)	(?) (?)	(?) (?)	
Upcards	♠ A	♦ K	♦ 8	
	♥ 10	♦ 4	♣ 7	Pot: $1.25

	HARRY	
Hole cards	(♠ J)	(♥ J)
Upcards	♠ 10	
	♥ 8	

Bob, who is still high, bets. Dick and Frank call. What should Harry do?

4. In Question 3, Harry calls. The third round of upcards leads to the following situation.

WIN AT POKER

	BOB	DICK	FRANK
Hole cards	(?) (?)	(?) (?)	(?) (?)
Upcards	♠ A	♦ K	♦ 8
	♥ 10	♦ 4	♣ 7
	♥ 3	♣ A	♥ Q

Pot: $2.25

	HARRY
Hole cards	(♠ J) (♥ J)
Upcards	♠ 10
	♥ 8
	♣ 10

Harry is now high and has a pair showing so the bet limit is doubled (to fifty cents). What should Harry do?

5. In Question 4, Harry checks. Bob also checks, but Dick bets fifty cents. Frank raises to $1! There is now $3.75 in the pot. What should Harry do?

SOLUTIONS

1. (a) Drop. Wait till next year. The straight possibility with low cards isn't worth a second glance.

(b) Drop. The three-card flush is more tempting, but the cards are woefully low and two hearts are already out.

(c) Drop. With just an ace your hand is no better than a little below average.

(d) Call. Here the ace has some strength to back it up and a straight possibility as well.

(e) Drop. Avoid playing low pairs, particularly with no concealment value. A split pair should be jacks or higher to justify a stay on the first round.

(f) Drop. Surprised? Then you didn't look at the upcards carefully enough. Both missing jacks are showing and you would be playing a "dead hand" if you called.

(g) Call. *This* split pair is worth a play.

(h) Call. While this is a much better hand than (g), there is no reason to take any other action. This is just a very good calling hand.

(i) Call. I don't like raising early in seven-card stud as a general principle. In particular, if you raise now, your opponents will make a mental note that you may have three threes. Better to wait and see how things develop, hoping for a killing.

(j) Call. This is a better type of hand on which to raise, for your opponents won't know where your strength lies. I consider a raise acceptable—it shows a good understanding of concealment—but I wouldn't do it.

2. Call. An easy one. Harry has a high pair, concealment, and good improvement possibilities.

3. Call. Harry now has only moderate values but his eight-spot opens up the possibility of a straight—a serious issue as no nines (and no queens and only one seven) have shown thus far.

4. I would check. At this stage, no one has reason to believe Harry has more than a possible straight. He can't have three tens (Bob has one and Ed folded one on the first round) so the others will not be afraid to bet. In this way, Harry can discover where the outstanding strength lies while retaining a chance for a big pot if he makes a full house.

5. Drop. Either Frank has three queens or he is pulling a big bluff. With Harry's open pair and Bob and Dick holding potential aces up and kings up, Frank is walking straight into the lion's den. Three queens is the obvious answer. No queens have been dealt as upcards and all Frank's plays

make sense if his two hole cards are queens. After all, he has been in roughly the same position as Harry if that is his holding.

This is not the time for Harry to call on the possibility that Frank is bluffing, for his position is bad—he has Bob and Dick to consider also. Dick, in particular, will be getting very good odds from the pot to call Frank's raise and will probably stay in.

Since Harry must assume he is beaten at this point, he must consider his chance of improvement and decide whether or not the pot offers suitable odds for a call. All the tens are out, so a jack is his only chance. Even if we assume that Bob, Dick, and Frank have hole cards which do not include a jack, the odds against Harry being dealt a jack for one of his last two cards are 6 to 1. The pot offers only about 4 to 1 at this point, so a call is unsound. Furthermore, Harry will not be assured of winning if he gets a jack. Frank has two chances to improve also.

The main point of this example is to be wary of the concealed hand. If an opponent bets strongly with a collection of junk for his upcards, start your thinking with what his original hole cards might have been.

E I G H T

◎ ◎ ◎ ◎ ◎

Wild Cards

Poker is a game of almost infinite variety. The many versions, however, are really modifications of the games of draw poker and stud poker which we have already discussed.

This book is intended as an introduction to poker and it is not possible to teach good strategy for as many different types of poker as could be crammed into its pages. Rather, I have presented guiding principles which can be applied to every poker form. Until you are experienced, try to avoid offshoots of the basic games. When you do feel ready to advance into the "poker jungle," you will need references which go beyond the scope of this book. Heed this warning. You will know quite a lot about the game of poker if you master the contents of this book. But every time you play a new form of poker, you must determine *how* your poker knowledge should be applied. Each poker variant involves new ideas, or new ways to apply familiar principles. Look before you leap.

The next few chapters are devoted to poker variations. Deep down inside, I have an uneasy feeling that these sections may prove the undoing of some readers as poker players. I fear that once you have learned the rules and absorbed my tidbits of advice, you will be unable to overcome the temptation to play these forms of poker. As it is likely that your preparation will be inadequate (how many of you, for example, will faithfully struggle through a proper observation phase before playing a new form?), you are likely to lose money in your early attempts. I beg of you to avoid this none too subtle trap. *Do not play any form of poker strange to you until you have read about it and observed it.*

Your first question should be: Why, if I recognize the dangers of presenting material on the more complicated forms of poker, do I include it in this book? There are several answers to that question. I hope they are good ones because I would feel guilty if this book were responsible for steering you along the wrong poker path. Here are my reasons:

(1) You may be reading this book out of intellectual curiosity, with no interest in playing the complicated forms of poker for significant stakes. Since the different poker variations are without doubt interesting, you would be deprived of part of the fascination of poker if I omitted them.

(2) There is some danger that you will wind up playing these new games anyway. It's better to know something about their operation and the principles that govern winning strategy than nothing at all about them.

(3) If you are going to play these games eventually, sooner or later you will need to learn their fundamentals. I can at least hope to provide you with a sound foundation for your later studies and explorations.

(4) You may not play poker for sizable stakes, but nonetheless you may be socially embarrassed by lack of knowledge of one or more of the poker forms favored by your group. A description of some of the more popular forms will

therefore be of use to you, even if you don't hope to turn the information into a monetary advantage.

(5) I'm not brave enough to omit the special forms solely on the theory that I am doing the reader a service. Who would believe me?

WHY POKER VARIATIONS WERE CREATED

Each poker variation was designed to overcome a deficiency in one of the earlier forms. (Thus, stud poker came into being primarily to provide more betting rounds than draw poker.) In many cases, sad to relate, new versions were introduced and championed by expert players who were looking for greener fields in which to practice their art. Aside from the fact that the paths of draw poker and stud poker are well beaten, so that the advantage of the expert over the novice lessens as time goes on, *the more complicated the game the greater the expert's advantage.*

This is one of the reasons I ask you to be wary of new games.

In this chapter I discuss **wild cards.** A wild card is a card that can be used as any card in the deck (even one held by the player using it). Wild cards were introduced because some players became tired of the relatively poor hands that resulted from the standard forms of draw and stud. Occasionally there is a good hand in draw poker, but you have to wait a long time to get it; in (five-card) stud poker, it is a rare event when anyone winds up with more than a pair or two.

By introducing wild cards, the range of likely hands is expanded. The amount of expansion depends on how many wild cards are used. Thus, the chance of seeing "good" hands (straights, flushes, etc.) is increased. Thus, one must readjust values. What was a good hand in ordinary poker may be worthless with wild cards in the game. Failure to adjust standards (by clinging stubbornly to a fixed idea of what is a good hand) is one of the most common failings of the inexperienced player when he moves from a normal game to one which includes wild cards.

But enough soapboxing—let's get down to business.

RULES FOR WILD-CARD GAMES

A wild card is a card which may be used as *any of the fifty-two ordinary cards.* I mention again, for it is worth repeating, that it is permissible to have a wild card stand for a card already held. If you have the ace of spades and a wild card in addition, you may name the wild card as a second ace of spades! The wild card takes on whatever value its holder assigns to it. If we let the symbol "W" stand for a wild card, a player with

$$W \quad \spadesuit A \quad \heartsuit J \quad \diamondsuit 10 \quad \clubsuit 3$$

would call his hand as a pair of aces. (It doesn't matter whether he calls the wild card the ace of spades or any other ace, the suits having no rank in poker.)

Sometimes, it *is* important to have the wild card stand for a specific card. Thus, with

$$W \quad \heartsuit 10 \quad \heartsuit 9 \quad \heartsuit 8 \quad \heartsuit 7$$

you should have the wild card stand for the jack of hearts, giving you a juicy straight flush. Also, with

Wild Cards

W   ♠ Q   ♠ 10   ♠ 8   ♠ 3

have the wild card represent the ace of spades. Any spade will give you a flush, so make the flush as high as possible. It is even possible to obtain that monstrosity, the "double-ace flush." Thus,

W   ♠ A   ♠ 10   ♠ 8   ♠ 3

is a double-ace flush in spades since you can designate the wild card as another ace of spades. Having two aces, the double-ace flush ranks above an ace-king flush. (And a triple-ace flush—possible with more than one wild card—outranks a mere double-ace flush.) Some groups, however, do not allow the double-ace flush, etc., and this matter should be discussed before play begins.

The inclusion of wild cards creates an entirely new rank: **five of a kind.** For example,

W   ♠ A   ♥ A   ♦ A   ♣ A

is "five aces" by having the wild card stand for an ace. Five of a kind ranks above a straight flush, so five aces is the highest possible hand. The following hands, which become possible if there is more than one wild card, are also five of a kind:

W	W	♥ K	♦ K	♣ K	(five kings)
W	W	W	W	♠ 6	(five sixes)
W	W	W	W	W	(five aces)

It is a common misconception that hands including wild cards are less valuable than hands which are made up wholly of "natural" cards. This has no basis in law. A wild card takes on every aspect and value of the card it represents. Thus, the following two hands are of *identical rank:*

W	♠ A	♥ K	♦ 10	♣ 2
♥ A	♦ A	♠ K	♣ 10	♥ 2

If no other player has better than a pair of aces, the players holding these hands would tie (and thus split the pot).

Which cards are wild depends upon the game chosen. In theory, it is possible to make any cards wild (see Chapter Ten for more on this subject) but in practice certain wild-card games are played widely while others are only local favorites. Wild cards which are popular (and discussed in this chapter) are **deuces** (deuces wild), the **joker** (a fifty-third card, supplied with most standard decks, which is added to the standard fifty-two-card pack), and the **bug** (also a fifty-third card—the so-called joker is usually added, but designated in advance as a bug). Variations played on occasion (not discussed here) include **one-eyed jacks wild** (the spade jack and heart jack have only one eye—take a look if you don't believe it), **all one-eyes wild** (the diamond king also suffers from this affliction), **deuces and one-eyed jacks wild,** and a virtually endless string of other combinations and complications.

DEUCES WILD

By far the most popular wild-card game is draw poker with deuces wild. Except for the stipulation that all four deuces act as wild cards, the game is identical to ordinary draw poker. If a player has a deuce, he must designate its significance when he exposes his cards in a showdown. No doubt deuces were chosen as wild cards because everyone thought he held a lot of them (everyone always has bad hands, and deuces are the lowest-ranking card when not wild). Funny how few deuces one holds when they are wild instead of lowly.

Having four wild cards in the game necessitates an enormous change in hand valuation. Whereas the average winning hand in ordinary draw poker is jacks-up, with deuces wild the average winner is three kings or three aces! A pair of kings, for example, is a pretty good hand in ordinary draw poker: usually worth a call, sometimes good enough for an opening bet. With deuces wild a pair of kings should almost always be relegated to the discard pile. (A pair of kings with a lowly deuce, on the other hand, is a horse with a different saddle.)

Before I discuss changes in hand valuation, I will present the overriding consideration in *all* wild-card games. Understanding this principle is worth any other two pieces of information about wild-card games—with big casino thrown in.

Fundamental Principle of Hand Valuation in Wild-Card Games: A hand including a wild card is of *greater* value than the same hand made up of natural cards.

One reason this principle is so important is that it is contrary to the psychological reaction of the vast majority of players. With two natural aces, people think they have something "real." Yet, *it is a far, far better thing to have an ace and a deuce!*

Why? First, because every deuce you have is one wild card that nobody else has. And therefore it is that much less likely that someone else will be able to make a hand better than yours. Second, your hand is always more flexible when it contains a wild card. Compare these two hands:

| (Hand One) | ♠ A | ♥ A | ♦ 8 | ♥ 7 | ♣ 3 |
| (Hand Two) | ♠ 2 (wild) | ♥ A | ♦ 8 | ♥ 7 | ♣ 3 |

With each of these hands, you will try to improve by drawing three cards to your pair of aces. Suppose you get lucky and pick a pair of fives. Hand One becomes aces up; but Hand Two is now three fives. Also, turning a bit optimistic, consider the result of picking up something such as ♥ K ♣ J ♦ 10. With Hand One, you still have a pair of aces, but Hand Two has become a straight (having the deuce stand for a queen). Another piece of luck you might have is picking up three hearts—not likely, but it does happen. Hand Two becomes a flush while Hand One is still a pair of aces.

Hand valuation. Possession of a deuce is so valuable that hands without a deuce are hardly worth discussing. It may seem a shame to throw away something like three sixes—a terrific hand to be dealt in ordinary draw poker—but I recommend giving no consideration to any natural hand lower than three jacks. Some authorities consider any three of a kind playable, so my requirement is relatively conservative. This is a good time to interject an admonishment which applies to all wild-card games: *be conservative.* It is always easier to overestimate than underestimate your values. If you are uncertain how good your hand is, *downgrade it.* It is a good idea to value conservatively in any complicated poker game, but it is especially important in wild-card games. (How can you tell how many wild cards your opponents have?)

I will give average requirements for various actions. Remember to alter them depending on your position, the tendencies of your opponents, the ratio of ante to opening bet, etc. (see pages 66–69).

I have already mentioned that natural hands ranking

below three jacks should be thrown away. However, hands with deuces take on extra value. I consider a deuce and an ace a sound opening in any position; similarly for three of a kind including a deuce. Hands run so high in this game that one must always be cautious of raises. The minimum raising requirement is two deuces or a full house. Even a full house can be a doubtful value if there is a lot of betting before the draw. Four of a kind is fairly common in this game.

Drawing Cards. A few special problems arise involving drawing when your hand contains one or more deuces. Here is a list of special draws. In each case, I give the mathematically best method of trying to improve your hand. Remember that there will be exceptions based on the fact that you are trying to beat a specific hand (see pages 87–88 for a discussion of this technique in ordinary draw poker).

Your Holding	*(Usually) Best Draw*
Two deuces	Keep an ace (or a pair, of course); otherwise draw three cards.
One deuce with:	
High pair (aces or kings) and open straight flush	Keep the pair and draw two.
Lower pair and open straight flush	Draw one to the straight flush.

JOKER DRAW POKER

When a joker is added to the deck as a fifty-third card, hand values do not change as radically as they do in deuces wild. (The average winning hand is three sevens or three eights.) Since only one player can have a wild card, it is easy to summarize the best strategy for this game.

(1) When you do not have the joker (which will be most of the time), value your hand lower than you would in ordinary draw poker. Up your requirements for opening, calling, raising, etc., by a notch or two, for someone else probably has a joker to help him make a good hand. (However, your valuation should not be as conservative as in deuces wild.)

(2) When you *do* have the joker, be wildly optimistic. Remember that *no one else can have a wild card*. The joker alone is worth a call on the opening round (though I don't recommend calling a raise unless it is backed up by an ace or a moderate pair) and certain innocent-looking combinations may well be worth a raise. You are more likely to improve

Joker   ♠ A   ♦ 10   ♥ 6   ♣ 3

than

♦ A   ♠ A   ♦ 10   ♥ 6   ♣ 3

because of the flexibility of the joker, and I consider ace-joker a raising hand. Some hands offer excellent improvement possibilities:

Joker   ♦ 10   ♥ 9   ♣ 8   ♦ 2

If you discard the ♦ 2, the draw of an eight, nine, or ten (9 possibilities) will give you three of a kind, while a queen, jack, seven, or six (16 possibilities) will give you a straight. Thus, the odds are 25 to 23 *in your favor* that you will wind up with no worse than three eights—a probable winning hand. And who knows, every so often you may draw an ace and win with a pair of aces!

Sometimes it is difficult to decide which cards to keep with the joker. In such a situation, consider each of the possibilities and count the number of cards that will help you in each case.

One final tip on draw poker with the joker: a bluff is far more likely to succeed when you have the joker than when you don't. Particularly when you have drawn one card, your opponents must fear that you held a combination such as the one discussed above which made you odds-on to draw a very good hand. Similarly, if you don't have the joker, be very cautious about bluffing. Almost certainly, one of your opponents has it, and not only will this tend to give him a good enough hand to call your bluff, he will know that you have no wild card yourself.

THE BUG

Sometimes the fifty-third card is designated as the *bug*, even though the playing card may be labeled as joker. The bug is a wild card which takes on special functions, its precise significance being determined by the form of poker being played. In draw poker, the bug may be designated as an ace, or a card needed to produce a flush or straight (or straight flush). Thus, we have the following:

Bug	♠ A	♥ Q	♦ 6	♣ 5	(pair of aces)
Bug	♠ A	♠ Q	♠ 6	♠ 5	(flush)
Bug	♠ Q	♦ J	♣ 10	♥ 9	(straight)

It should be noted that the bug does not function as a full joker. Compare the following:

Bug ♥ K ♦ Q ♣ 10 ♠ 6	Joker ♥ K ♦ Q ♣ 10 ♠ 6
(ace-king high)	(pair of kings)
Bug ♠ A ♦ 10 ♣ 10 ♠ 2	Joker ♠ A ♦ 10 ♣ 10 ♠ 2
(aces up)	(three tens)

Clearly the bug is not nearly as valuable as the joker. Because of this, many poker groups which enjoy the use of a wild card to enliven the game are switching from the joker to the bug. Draw poker with the bug retains the flavor of wild-card games without giving an overwhelming advantage to the player lucky enough to hold the wild card.

Smaller though that advantage may be, one must still tread warily when the bug is in play. Be especially cautious when your values are not in aces—remember that there are five "aces" in the deck and only four of everything else. Thus, a pair of aces and a pair of kings are no longer next-door neighbors: they live far apart because of the added chance to improve the aces. In fact, until you are an experienced player, you will do well not to call in a deal of bug draw with less than a pair of aces.

When you hold the bug, the picture is rosy. If nothing else, you know that no one else holds it. Again you may be called on to count the number of ways you can improve with various draws. With

Bug   ♠ K   ♠ 9   ♠ 8   ♥ 7

you should discard the king, trying to draw a straight (16 possibilities) rather than the higher-ranking flush (only 10 possibilities). Since no one else has a wild card, a straight should be good enough to win almost all the time.

Don't fall into the trap of thinking you are obligated to stay in when you have the bug. Remember, the bug is *not* as good as a joker. With a collection such as

Wild Cards

Bug	♥ Q	♦ 10	♠ 7	♣ 4

you have no reason to call a bet before the draw.

STUD POKER WITH WILD CARDS

With a few exceptions (notably baseball—see page 179, and low hole card wild) wild cards are generally not used in stud poker. The reason is that the introduction of wild cards would have a stultifying effect on the game. As soon as anyone was dealt a wild upcard, the other players would be almost certain to drop out, thus ending the pot.

Should you become involved with a group that uses a wild-card variation of stud poker, however, two simple rules will be helpful:

(1) If there is only one wild card, assume it is the hole card of the player who takes the lead in the betting.

(2) If there are four (or more) wild cards, such as in deuces-wild stud poker, virtually never play without a wild card and assume that each of your opponents who stays for several cards has one in the hole.

As in all wild-card games, conservatism should be the order of the day.

The quiz that follows emphasizes situations which bring out the differences between wild-card and other games, and special techniques for operating with wild cards.

QUIZ

Our typical eightsome is still battling, at the usual stakes, but has generously switched to wild-card games in honor of this chapter.

1. Draw poker with deuces wild. Harry deals; Al checks; Bob opens; Charlie and Dick call; Ed, Frank, and George drop. What action should Harry take with each of the following hands?

(a)	♠ A	♥ A	♦ 10	♣ 8	♥ 6
(b)	♣ J	♦ J	♥ 7	♠ 7	♦ 3
(c)	♠ 2	♠ A	♦ K	♣ 9	♠ 3
(d)	♠ 2	♠ A	♠ K	♠ 10	♥ 7
(e)	♠ 2	♥ 2	♦ 10	♥ 6	♣ 3

2. Draw poker with a joker. The betting does not lead you to suspect that any of your opponents holds an outstanding hand. You must draw cards first. How do you draw to each of the following hands?

(a)	Joker	♠ A	♦ K	♥ 9	♣ 6
(b)	Joker	♠ A	♦ K	♥ 6	♣ 6
(c)	Joker	♦ 10	♣ 9	♦ 8	♦ 2
(d)	Joker	♥ Q	♠ Q	♠ J	♠ 10
(e)	Joker	♥ 7	♠ 7	♠ 6	♠ 5

3. Draw poker with the bug. After three checks, the pot is opened by the player on your right. You raise. The player on your left and the opener call, everyone else dropping out. The opener draws three cards. How do you draw to each of the following hands?

(a)	Bug	♠ A	♦ J	♣ 10	♥ 6
(b)	Bug	♠ A	♦ K	♦ 6	♥ 4
(c)	♠ A	♦ A	♦ 5	♣ 5	♥ 2
(d)	Bug	♥ 7	♥ 6	♠ 5	♥ 2

Wild Cards

1. (a) Drop. With three players in, there are probably a lot of deuces floating around. A pair of aces is not the same good value it is in ordinary draw poker.

(b) Drop. In a way, this hand is worse than aces. Neither (a) nor (b) figures to win unimproved, and the odds against improving two pairs are enormous—not nearly matched by the odds in the pot. Further, there is no guarantee that a full house will win. You have no wild cards; one of your opponents (presumably the opener as there were no raises) may have *two*. (Compare with discussion of the strength of a pair of aces because of improvement possibilities, page 97, and recall the odds against improving two pairs to a full house, page 89. Even with four wild cards available to be drawn, the odds do not change much because there is a presumption that the other players in the pot hold some or all of the wild cards.)

(c) Call. This is a better hand than (a) for several reasons. You have one deuce that your opponents do not and your chance of significant improvement is much greater.

(d) Raise. This action is based mainly on your good position for the purpose of drawing cards. After you see how many cards your callers draw, you can decide whether to draw three cards to the deuce-ace or (more likely) throw away the heart seven and try for a straight flush (5 chances), flush (7 additional chances), straight (6 additional chances), three aces (3 additional chances), or three kings (3 additional chances).

(e) Raise. Your possession of two deuces decreases the chance that your opponents have wild cards. Two deuces are worth a raise in most circumstances even when, as here, there is nothing in support and three cards must be drawn.

2. (a) Three cards to joker-ace. It is against the odds to keep the king. The chance of drawing a straight is very slight.

(b) Two cards to joker-six-six. There is no reason for any other draw, except possibly to confuse the enemy.

(c) One card to joker-ten-nine-eight, rather than try for the flush by throwing away the ♣ 9. Either way your chance of drawing three of a kind is the same. However, you have 16 ways of making a straight (queens, jacks, sevens, and sixes) and only 10 ways of making a flush (diamonds). Either improvement should win, so give yourself the best chance of improving.

(d) Usually two cards to joker-queen-queen. If you discard the heart queen, there are 22 cards you can draw which will give you a better hand than three queens. So your chance of improving is almost a 50-50 proposition. But three queens will probably win the pot at least half the time without improvement, and there is still a chance to draw a queen or a pair if you discard ♠ J ♠ 10. I would keep the straight-flush possibility only with good reason to believe that three queens was not the best hand before the draw.

(e) This is the same situation as in (d), except that now it is less likely that you will win the hand with an unimproved three sevens. In this case, there is more reason to try for the straight flush. One reason in favor of breaking up the triplets—not mentioned above when I was plugging for keeping them—is that if you draw a new three of a kind (by picking up a six or a five or even a new seven) you will have more or less the same hand you started with and will have lost nothing.

3. (a) Three to the bug-ace. If you try for the straight (by throwing away the ♥ 6) the odds against your making it are 5 to 1. But since there are five aces in the deck, the odds against your improving significantly by drawing three cards

to the bug-ace are not 2½ to 1 (as in the case of drawing to a pair of aces in regular draw, see page 89) but less than 2 to 1.

(b) I would try two cards to bug-ace-king. It is likely that opener has aces. I would play to beat him with the kicker. If the man behind you has two pairs, you will probably win with aces up, and keeping a kicker does not diminish your chances of making two pairs.

(c) One card to the two pairs. Even though there is an "extra ace" in the deck, it doesn't pay to break up two pairs to give yourself a better chance at three aces. Anyway, one of your opponents may have the bug.

(d) Discard the ♥ 2, trying for a straight. For purposes of this problem, the situation is identical to that in question 2(c).

NINE

◎ ◎ ◎ ◎ ◎

Low and High-Low
Poker

Every poker player believes he holds worse cards than anyone else. It is easy, therefore, to see the motivation for **low poker**—in which all the usual rules of poker apply except that the player with the *lowest*-ranked poker hand in the showdown wins the pot.

Low poker (draw, stud, with or without wild cards or extra cards) is excellent as a change of pace and has the generally unrecognized feature that differences in skill are less meaningful in terms of results than in the other popular forms of poker. This is not to say that skill does not count for more than luck (it does), nor that the best players will not usually win (they will). However, if Player A has the same advantage in knowledge and technique over Player B in both high and low poker, player A will win less at low poker if the games are played for comparable stakes.

In the interests of simplicity, most poker groups carry over the procedures of high poker to low poker without exception. Unfortunately, this apparently logical transition introduces an anomaly. At stud poker, the man with the *highest* combination in his upcards is forced to act first within each betting round. This is illogical at low stud, for it is grossly unfair to give the worst betting position to the player with the worst (i.e., highest) hand. Instead, I recommend that when stud poker is played for low, the obligation to speak first within each betting round devolve upon the player whose upcards form the *lowest-valued* (and thus potentially best) poker combination.

Another technical problem of low poker revolves around the status of aces, straights, and flushes. We have seen (page 11) that the ace is considered as either a high card or a low card when it comes to forming a straight. Thus, both of the following are straights:

| A | K | Q | J | 10 | (highest straight) |
| 5 | 4 | 3 | 2 | A | (lowest straight) |

Since the ace is awarded dual status in this regard, the question arises whether or not the ace should also be considered as a low card for purposes of low poker. In other words, should

$$8 \quad 6 \quad 4 \quad 3 \quad A$$

be higher (if ace is high only) or lower (if ace may be low) than

$$8 \quad 6 \quad 4 \quad 3 \quad 2$$

If the ace must be high, the first hand is only "ace low," whereas it is an "eight low" if the ace may be treated as a low card.

Another question involves holdings such as

♠ 7 ♥ 6 ♦ 5 ♥ 4 ♣ 3

and

♥ 8 ♥ 6 ♥ 5 ♥ 4 ♥ 2

These hands look like candidates for good lows ("seven-six" low and "eight-six" low respectively) but the first is a straight and the second a flush. If the straight and flush retain their rank as (relatively) high hands, these hands have virtually no value in low poker.

The modern trend in poker is to treat aces, straights, and flushes as *either high or low at their holder's option*. In other words, *straights and flushes do not count*. Thus, the lowest possible hand is 5-4-3-2-A (often called a wheel or a bicycle). Note that if aces, straights, and flushes are high only, the lowest possible hand is 7-5-4-3-2 (not all the same suit).

There is a sound technical reason for treating aces, straights, and flushes as *either* high or low, and I recommend this rule highly. The reason is that it adds tremendous interest to high-low poker, presently considered the ultimate form of the game. Notice also that the "player's option" rule is consistent with the rule that an ace may represent a rank lower than deuces in the straight 5-4-3-2-A (in high poker). Thus, allowing aces, straights, and flushes to swing, that is, to be high or low at their holder's option, provides for a consistent valuation of hands whether the game is high, low, or high-low, and increases the enjoyment and excitement of several forms of poker. The reverse rule has nothing more than tradition to recommend it and is thus a poor second to the modern treatment. In this chapter, we assume that aces may be considered low and straights and flushes do not count.

Low and High-Low Poker

1. Stud poker for low.

At first glance, it may seem surprising that *six*-card stud is becoming the most popular form of this game. But this trend is quite a rational one: five-card stud leads to few good low hands, for it is so easy to catch one bad card (picture card, or card making a pair) out of five. On the other hand, with *seven* cards it is all too easy to make a good low hand. So six-card stud is the logical compromise.

One rule will give you a good head start toward playing low stud. In the early stages, regardless of the odds offered by the pot, drop as soon as you receive a bad card (any card ten or higher or a card that gives you a pair) unless *every* opponent also has a bad card.

If you remember this rule you will do reasonably well in low stud.

For reasons which psychologists have not yet determined—and the failure of the major foundations to establish grants for such studies is truly astonishing—low-stud games tend to involve wild, if not frivolous, betting. This is perhaps caused by the fact—and it is a fact—that no matter how far behind you are, you can catch up, if your opponent draws one bad card. True enough, but always bear in mind that poker is a game of percentages. Stay conservative at low stud and you are a guaranteed winner in a typical (loose) game.

For those of you who may be tempted into the low arena, here is some specific advice on low-stud strategy. These remarks assume that either five-card or six-card stud is being played. Also, I assume that aces, straights and flushes may be considered low. (If otherwise, minor adjustments must be made.)

(1) Don't stay on the first round without a "perfect" hole

card (A, 2, 3, 4, or 5, with no pair) unless both your cards are lower than all the other upcards.

(2) In the early rounds, don't play if you receive a bad card (ten or higher, or a pair) unless *everyone* else also has a bad card.

(3) After the early rounds, assume each opponent has a perfect hole card.

(4) If you are only slightly behind, the odds against your overtaking a better hand are only 2 to 1. At the later stages, the pot usually offers better odds.

Here is an application of rule (4). At six-card low stud, you are faced with this situation:

Opponent	You
(?)	(♦ 3)
♠ 4	♣ 4
♦ 7	♠ 6
♠ A	♥ 2
♥ Q	♠ K

Your opponent (with the low board) now bets fifty cents, bringing the pot to $2, and no other players are active. Even though you are almost surely beaten, you should call. The odds against your coming out with a better hand are not as high as the 4 to 1 offered by the pot.

2. Draw poker for low (lowball).

Although of recent vintage, lowball is probably the most popular form of low poker. It is especially popular in club games on the West Coast.

I advise the inexperienced player to be wary of lowball. It would seem that a listing of values necessary for opening, calling, raising, etc.—as was given for high draw poker— would suffice to get you off to a good start. But this is not quite so, for two reasons. First, lowball is highly unusual in that good play requires a knowledge of principles that do not apply to other forms of poker. Second, lowball is a fast-moving game. It takes direct observation merely to determine the true stakes. Money management and poker overhead present special problems.

In short, lowball is not a game for the uninitiated. If you are a newcomer to low poker, stick to stud until you have mastered the values of low. Only then should you proceed to the more arduous task of learning how to play lowball. And when you do, bear in mind that the general principles you have learned will apply less forcefully to lowball than any other common form of poker.

Lack of space prevents anything approaching a complete discussion of lowball, but I will present an introduction to hand valuation and basic strategy.

(1) *Before the draw.* Lowball is a game of possibilities and you should open or call with four cards to a six low or better, intending to draw one card. The only pat hands worth considering are eight low or better. (While a nine low, say, will probably be best before the draw, there will usually be several callers drawing one to a good low. One of them will probably come up with a better hand than nine-low.) No hand requiring a two-card draw should be played. A raise should be based on a pat seven-low or better, or occasionally four to a wheel. When the bug is used (see next section), three low cards with the bug is worth a raise.

(2) *The draw.* The only problem posed by the draw is whether you should break up a moderate hand to try for a very good hand. For example, with 9 4 3 2 A, you have a choice between standing pat and drawing one card. This decision should be based on the number of opponents. With only one or two opponents, I would keep the nine low. (This particular hand will be lower than all other nine lows.)

However, with more than two opponents, the chances are that one of them will draw a better hand, so you should throw the nine and hope to improve. Also, if one of your opponents stays pat in front of you, he probably has you beaten (especially if he has bet strongly), and again you should throw away the nine.

(3) *After the draw.* Betting after the draw depends largely on position. If you are last to speak, you can call (or even bet) on moderate values because the pot usually offers very good odds and there is a good chance that others have **busted** (drawn a bad card). However, in bad position, you should check almost regardless of your values (hoping to build the pot when you have a good hand) if you have the opportunity, and avoid calling on moderate values if there is more than one player to speak behind you, for the chance of a raise is considerable.

(4) *Hand values.* The average winning hand is about 8-5 low, but this is not a *typical* winner because some deals are won with very poor hands (several players having drawn one card and busted). A seven low is a potential winner and a six low is worth taking the lead in the betting after the draw in the absence of unusually strong betting by an opponent.

3. Low poker with wild cards.

Low poker is rarely played with more than one wild card. With too many wild cards, there are a lot of perfect hands floating around, leading to ties (and even multiple ties) which decrease interest in the game.

When one wild card is used, it is usually an extra (fifty-third) card and designated as the bug—though joker would be an equally appropriate designation. The bug may be designated as a card of any rank not held. Thus,

8   6   5   4   Bug

would be an eight-six low, the bug being designated as an ace;

$$7 \quad 5 \quad 2 \quad A \quad Bug$$

would be a seven-five low, the bug representing a three.

The bug is extremely powerful in low poker for it is automatically of good value, decreases the chance of getting paired, and increases the number of cards which will help the hand. For example, with

$$5 \quad 4 \quad 3 \quad 2$$

you require an ace to complete a wheel, but with

$$5 \quad 4 \quad 3 \quad Bug$$

you will have a wheel if you get *either* an ace or a deuce.

HIGH-LOW POKER

I mentioned above that most poker enthusiasts regard high-low as the ultimate form of the game. This method of poker play is replacing all other forms in serious games and is already nearly universal in expert games.

The basic principle of high-low poker is that in the showdown the players with the highest and lowest poker hands divide the pot equally. Thus high-low combines high poker and low poker. It is in high-low that the skill factor in poker is at its highest; this explains why it is a favorite of expert players.

The main feature of high-low which makes skill pay off (and also makes it so hard to learn to play successfully) is that the slightest change in the mechanics of the game can have a tremendous effect on strategy. Thus, to take a highly simplified example, in high-low *five*-card stud it is generally best to play for high at the beginning, whereas in high-low *seven*-card stud, one should usually play for low in the early stages. Values are often deceptive: in high-low draw poker, one should wait for a *better* high hand than necessary in high poker or a *better* hand than necessary in low poker in order to open, call, raise, and so forth. Thus, it does *not* suffice to combine knowledge of both the high and low forms in order to come up with a formula for successful play at high-low.

Furthermore, high-low poker introduces a completely new aspect: declarations. In some (but not all) versions the players must declare whether they wish to try for the high half of the pot, the low half of the pot, *or both*. On top of this, there are several methods of declaration, and proper tactics vary widely with the form of declaration.

I have included this description of high-low poker to give you an idea of its complexities. High-low is out of bounds for the inexperienced player. This is an absolute prohibition. You are forbidden to play high-low (except in a social game or for practice, and then only at nominal stakes). At least, I take on no responsibility for your results.

If you develop a keen interest in poker—which is likely since you have read this far—you will eventually become fascinated by high-low poker. This is to be expected, as there is little question that high-low is the most intriguing form of the game. When this occurs, you must exercise great restraint and not play in—or even watch—high-low games until you have fully mastered the simpler forms of poker *and have read extensively about high-low strategy.*

There are many stages of development which you must pass through before you will be ready to attempt high-low poker. The poker principles and techniques presented in this book will, I hope, give you a firm foundation. But do not think that these pages will provide you with all you need to know to start your high-low career. It would take another book of this size just to get you started.

Building your poker repertoire requires patience.

FORMS OF HIGH-LOW POKER

I should require an affidavit to the effect that you will not play high-low poker without adequate preparation before I allow you to read this section; alas, it is impractical. You are therefore released on your own recognizance.

The most important feature of a high-low form is the method used in the showdown. The simplest method, **cards speak** (a shortening of the poker expression "The cards speak for themselves"), is similar to that used in other games. In cards speak, each player in the showdown exposes his hand and selects his best five cards for high and his best five cards for low. When only five cards are dealt, there is no choice involved. However, high-low often involves extra cards. With more than five cards to choose from, a player may use any five for his high and any five for his low—the same cards need not be used. For example, if you have:

♠ A ♦ A ♥ 10 ♣ 10 ♥ 5 ♣ 4 ♠ 3

in a seven-card game, you have aces-up for high (using the two aces, the two tens, and the five) and a ten low for low (using 10-5-4-3-A).

The players with the highest and lowest hands divide the pot equally. (If there is an odd chip it is traditional to give it to the high winner, though some groups add it to the ante for the next pot.) Should one player win both high and low, he wins the entire pot. In case of a tie in either "direction," that half of the pot is divided among the players involved in the tie. For example, if A wins high with B and C tying for low, A gets half the pot, B and C each get a quarter of the pot.

Cards speak is by far the simpler of the two basic forms of high-low and thus much the easier to learn to play successfully. You should not even consider playing the other form (declaration) until you have had considerable experience at the easier game.

Declaration, or high-low with declarations, has many different variations. The new ingredient in this dish is that each player in the showdown must declare whether he wishes to try for the high half of the pot, the low half of the pot, *or both*. It might seem there is no reason not to try for both portions of the pot, but the risk is serious indeed. For if a player declares both high and low, and is defeated in *either* attempt, he loses his rights to the other half of the pot. In other words, declaring high-low is an all-or-nothing gamble.

Choosing your declaration is as difficult a task as all other poker considerations put together. You can know everything about hand values, betting strategy, and so forth, but if you don't choose declarations effectively, nothing will prevent you from sustaining heavy losses.

High-low with declarations breaks down into two forms: **simultaneous declaration** and **consecutive declaration**. In simultaneous declaration, each player in the showdown indicates his choice by secretly concealing an appropriate marker (usually a coin or chip) in his closed fist. When each participant has made his decision, and thus each has a closed fist up on the table, all the declarations are revealed simultaneously. In consecutive declaration, the players declare in order, beginning with a designated player. Here again there are numerous variations. Some groups begin with the first player left of the dealer's seat; some with the last player to raise, or the last to open a round of betting if there was no raise; in high-low stud, where there are upcards, sometimes the player with the highest-showing poker combination must declare first, sometimes the player with the lowest. (Obviously, it is an enormous advantage to declare last, or as close to last as possible. This is a positional advantage which outweighs all other positional advantages we have discussed in this book.)

However the declarations are accomplished, the pot is divided into two halves. The high half goes to the player with the highest hand *among those declaring for high;* the low half to the player with the lowest hand *among those declaring for low.* It is possible for a player to declare for and win both halves of the pot, but bear in mind that if he does not win both he can win neither.

Whether cards speak or declaration is used in the showdown, high-low may be played in any of the common poker forms. High-low draw poker is most common with five cards, but is sometimes played with six or seven; a variation gaining popularity is to allow *two* draws (with a round of betting in between) instead of the usual one; another twist is to play high-low draw with a common card exposed in the center, as in spit in the ocean (see page 180). High-low stud poker is most common with seven cards, but is frequently played with only five or six. Games such as baseball and anaconda (as well as other dealer's choice games, see Chapter Ten) are frequently played high-low. Except for the dealer's choice games, however, wild cards are generally not used in high-low.

You can see from this description that there are at least

two hundred basic forms of high-low poker, even if we don't count local variations. The single most popular form is seven-card stud with declarations. Consecutive declaration is the traditional method in the showdown but is gradually being replaced (especially in expert games) by simultaneous declaration, which is by far the superior form.

Seven-card-stud high-low with declarations is the game you will eventually want to play if you become a serious poker player.

HIGH-LOW STRATEGY

It is difficult to give advice on high-low tactics without considering each different form individually. The slightest change in rules may cause a considerable shift in the most desirable course to follow. I think it will be more valuable (to those of you who will progress to high-low poker) if I present those elements of high-low strategy which can successfully be applied to all (or at least most) forms of the game. Accordingly, the high-low advice below will be general in nature.

1. Hand values and pot odds. It is of the utmost importance to realize that unless you have a chance to obtain a hand which will win *both* directions, you are betting to win only *half* the pot. Accordingly, the pot odds will generally be only half as great as they would be in a **one-way game** (high only or low only). While this feature does not mean you need "twice as good a hand" in your direction than you needed in a one-way game in order to open, bet, call, raise, etc. (because not everyone in the pot will be trying to make the same type of hand as you), it does indicate that you need a considerably better high hand (or a considerably better low hand) to make the same bets that you would need to do so in a one-winner game.

Therefore, do not fall into the error of applying the same standards from high and low games to high-low. Wait for much better values in the direction you are attempting.

2. Two-way hands. A hand that offers possibilities for both high and low is usually superior, for it offers more ways to improve. For example, a holding such as 5-4-3 in high-low stud is a good start—you have three cards towards a perfect (5-4-3-2-A) low and also a chance to make a straight. The *best* hands are those that can be turned into **two-way winners**, that is, can be used to win both halves of the pot. Unless more than five cards are dealt, such hands usually involve the two-way possibilities discussed on page 160: aces, straights, and flushes. Thus, a wheel, 5-4-3-2-A, has the virtue of being a straight as well as a perfect low.

A basic application of the two-way principle occurs in high-low stud, cards speak, when played with five cards, and, to a lesser extent, when played with six cards. *It is almost never correct to stay in the early rounds of this game unless you have an ace.* The reason is that no hand lacking an ace is likely to win both high and low. However, if you have an ace, you may easily gather in the entire pot, even with ordinary cards. Consider these two final hands at five-card high-low, cards speak.

(A)	♣ K	♥ J	♦ 8	♣ 7	♥ 3
(B)	♦ A	♦ Q	♥ 10	♠ 7	♣ 4

If players with hands (A) and (B) enter a showdown, the player with (B) will win both high and low. He has an ace high for high (against only a king high) and has a queen low (against a king low).

The ace also gives protection against losing both directions. In the same game, if you have five unmatched cards which include an ace, and are opposed by only one opponent, *you cannot be defeated in both directions.*

(Note: These considerations do *not* apply with equal force to declaration games because of the necessity to commit oneself before seeing the opponents' cards.)

Do not be intrigued by a hand which might be turned into either a high or a low if it is not much of either after a few cards. For example, if in seven-card high-low stud your first five cards are

♠ 9   ♥ 9   ♦ 6   ♦ 5   ♦ 2

you have a pair, a possible good low, a possible straight, and a possible flush. But when you add it all up it turns out that you have nothing much of anything at present. You will need two goods cards to make a good high or two good cards to make a good low (a nine low, assuming you make one, is usually not good enough to win). *Don't bet on possibilities after the first few cards.* If you play hands such as this, you will find yourself with the second-best high and the second-best low in many showdowns. There is no consolation prize for second.

3. Don't "chase" a possible two-way winner.

Be wary of situations in which you are betting to win back your own money. If two players battle each other down to the wire and then split the pot, they profit only to the extent of the money put in by others in the early stages. Consider this situation at seven-card stud, cards speak.

	Opponent X	You
Hole	(?)	(♥ Q)
cards	(?)	(♥ K)
Upcards	♦ 6	♣ K
	♥ 5	♠ K

Low and High-Low Poker

Prior to the dealing of the second round of upcards there is $1 in the pot. You are high board with a pair of kings showing and check, hoping to draw several players trying for low into the pot. Unfortunately, opponent X bets fifty cents and everyone else drops. What should you do?

You should drop also. The pot now contains $1.50. By calling, you stand to win fifty cents (half the new pot of $2 minus the fifty cents you must put in to call). But in order to have the chance to win this fifty cents you must call fifty cents now and fifty cents further after each of the remaining cards. It will cost you $2 to see the hand through, just to try to win that fifty cents. Opponent X has a sure winner for low *and may be able to make a straight and beat you for high.* True, you may obtain a full house, but why lay 4-to-1 odds against yourself?

4. Build the pot when everyone else is going the other way.

The opposite situation to that described in the previous example occurs when you are assured of winning in one direction and there are two or more players fighting it out for the other. In this case, it is to your advantage to build the pot at every opportunity. Your winnings will depend upon how much one of the opponents can be tempted into losing.

5. Don't fight for half the pot on even terms.

Suppose a situation such as the one in (4.) exists: A is assured of winning low; B and C each has a potential good high. If you are B or C, get out as quickly as possible (especially if your betting position is bad, i.e., if you speak immediately after A—who will always raise, putting you in the middle). If you have, let us say, an equal chance against the man you are fighting, your equity is 50 percent *of half the pot,* or 25 percent. But from now on you will be putting in 33 percent of the money. Unless the amount already bet by other players will make up for this difference (and it often won't, for player A is going to keep raising), *get out fast.*

I have listed only a few of the precepts of successful high-low strategy, but they will provide you with clues as to what to look for when you begin your observation of high-low poker.

TEN

◎ ◎ ◎ ◎ ◎

Dealer's Choice

With all the different poker variations to choose from, deciding the form of poker to be played is a difficult (though not unpleasant) task for a poker group. Generally, this issue is decided in one of two ways. If the group agrees on one, or possibly two or three, poker forms, these will be the only games played. Often, this will be specified as "draw poker," or "draw poker with deuces wild every other round," (a round consists of one deal by each player, so that the deal makes a complete circle around the table) or "five-card stud with an occasional round of draw," or whatever the group prefers. Although most poker players are happy with any of the basic forms, there are some who have special favorites which may not meet with general approval. When such a situation arises, it is usual to settle the matter by invoking the dealer's choice rule.

Under dealer's choice, the player whose turn it is to deal determines the form of poker to be played. This gives each player a chance to play his favorite game, and no one can complain for everyone has the same rights. Frequently, the choice of games is restricted to a short list found "acceptable" by the group. Most of the games discussed in detail in this book will be acceptable to any poker group. Occasionally, the dealer is allowed to name *any* poker game. Nonstandard games which may be chosen by the dealer have thus come to be called dealer's choice games. These will be discussed later in the chapter.

The choice rule introduces one difficulty. We have seen (Chapter Five) that the dealer has an inherent advantage in games of draw poker. It would be unfair to give an "edge" to the man who names draw poker as his favorite game—at least, it would be unfair to those who prefer stud—so it is necessary to make use of a **buck**. A buck is a marker which moves clockwise around the table and advances one position each time a hand of draw poker is played. The buck marks the person who is *assumed to be the dealer* for purposes of applying the rules of draw poker, regardless of who actually dealt the cards. The player thus designated is sometimes called the **draw dealer**. Poker history is largely a matter of legend, but it appears that the buck is as old as draw poker itself, and it is tempting to believe that poker is the source of the expression "passing the buck."

One of my own favorite rules simplifies dealer's choice and also does away with the need to use a buck. I find it bothersome to readjust my thinking to a new game after each and every deal. Therefore, when playing in a dealer's choice game, I recommend that each player in turn be granted the right to determine the form of poker played *for one round*. Everyone has the same rights as before, but time spent explaining (and reëxplaining to Sam, who went for a drink while the cards were being dealt) the game being played is cut down and the need for a buck—always a potential source of arguments—disappears.

When you become involved in a dealer's choice situation, your choice of game should depend on your immediate objective. If you are playing to win, you will naturally choose your "best game." Sometimes you will pick a game you have done well at during this particular session. On occasion, particularly during your learning period, you may opt for a game you are trying to learn, or gain experience playing. Otherwise, you simply pick the game you enjoy most. Choice of games is a good opportunity to build up your "nice guy" reputation (see page 20). Often it will not matter much to you which game is chosen. Therefore, you should avoid choosing a game which is unpopular with one or more members in the group.

Poker is most satisfactory when the stakes of all games played during a session are kept comparable. When the choice of games is restricted to the standard forms, this can be accomplished by adjusting the betting limits at stud to about one-quarter of the limits used for draw (see page 101). When the dealer is given a free hand in selecting the game to be played, it may be hard to judge how the stakes should be varied. I suggest using the *number of betting rounds* as the surest guide to the "size" of the game, and using this number to adjust the stakes by comparing it with the number of betting rounds in draw poker (2) and five-card stud (4).

Many of the nonstandard games are distinctly "weird" to the poker player who is unfamiliar with them. For this reason, it is a common error to treat an unfamiliar game as just so much nonsense. This error is a serious one. *Every poker variation is a game of skill.* I have examined and analyzed hundreds of different dealer's choice games and formulated principles of play for all but one. Think about that. Out of hundreds of games—far more than you or I will ever meet in practical play in a lifetime—only one* seemed to defy analysis. And it is quite possible that someone else *has* determined a superior strategy at this game.

---

* Seven-card stud, rank of low hole card wild for each player.

While the amount of skill and the effect of superior play will vary from game to game, it is essential to realize that far removed from the standard forms or not, each dealer's choice game can be analyzed in terms of basic poker principles (money management, hand values, position, overhead, psychology, odds, etc.). True, there are certain special principles which must be added to the usual list when unusual games are played. Nonetheless, you must treat these games as seriously as any other form of poker if you want to win. You should start your analysis of a new game by observing the average winning hand, the odds usually offered by the pot at various stages, and the tendencies of the players involved. Eventually, you will be able to determine your own set of hand values and will be off to a good start in developing your strategy for this game. Needless to say, these values will often depend as much on the players in the game and their tendencies as on the game itself.

Whatever the game, it is a safe rule that if it is unfamiliar to you your basic strategy should be *conservative*. There are several reasons for this: all players tend to be too optimistic whatever the game; most unusual games increase the chance of getting a good hand, so one must downgrade the usual values; you need invest realtively little money during your period of adjusting to the new game; conservatism is a good poker policy anyway.

In this chapter, I present and briefly discuss three dealer's choice games. I have chosen these games for the following reasons: first, they are among the most popular of the hundreds of known poker variations; second, they illustrate the scope of special games, encompassing draw poker, stud poker, combinations of the draw and stud principles, and even completely new ideas; third, they illustrate some of the most popular special gadgets frequently involved in these games.

Dealer's Choice

The games I discuss are:

BASEBALL: a stud game involving a large number of wild cards, the dealing of "extras," and unusual betting rules;

SPIT IN THE OCEAN: a draw game emphasizing the use of "common" cards;

ANACONDA: a combination of draw and stud which includes the passing of cards and the "roll-your-own principle."

The unusual games such as those described below are seldom played in serious games, and rarely for high stakes. Also, they are less dangerous than other new games because it is unlikely you will run into many people who know how to play them well. Nonetheless, you should still avoid playing a new poker form before both reading about it and watching it played. The tips on the games discussed below should be considered as additions to the basic poker principles which should always guide your play.

BASEBALL

When baseball is played with bat and ball, there are nine on a side and nine innings; also, there are three strikes to a batter and three outs to an inning; finally, after four balls you get a free base. Baseball with playing cards also makes use of the numbers nine, three, and four. It is stud poker (either five-card or seven-card) in which all nines and threes are wild, and the receipt of a four-spot as an upcard entitles its owner immediately to receive an extra card (an upcard in the five-card game, a hole card in the seven-card game). An additional twist is that if a three-spot is dealt as an upcard, its recipient must immediately (before any further cards are dealt) *match the pot or drop!*

The most significant feature of baseball from the point of

view of practical play is the gigantic number of wild cards. This, plus the occasional extra cards that are strewn around, causes lots of very good hands to come up. In the five-card game, the average winning hand is three aces; in the seven-card game it is *five* sixes.

In the early rounds, you should not play without a wild card or two, and any opponent who bets strongly should be placed with a minimum of one wild card in the hole.

When you are called upon to match the pot, remember that although it is tempting to keep that extra wild card, you are being called upon to make an even-money bet by matching. Therefore, you must be *odds-on* to win the pot at that point. In the seven-card game, it is almost impossible to get these odds early in the deal; in the five-card game, do not match the pot unless you will then be *well* ahead of everyone, even if every one of your opponents has a wild card in the hole! In the seven-card version, it may help you to remember that nothing short of five aces is ever a *sure* winner—and even then you may only tie. You should not be in the pot in the later stages with anything less than four aces, unless you have an especially good chance to make a five of a kind that figures to win and the pot offers very good odds. The latter may occur if someone matched the pot later than the first round.

SPIT IN THE OCEAN

"Spit," as this game is nicknamed, is a draw-poker game in which each player receives only four cards. However, this deficit is remedied by the turning of a **common card**, a card assumed to be part of everyone's hand. Furthermore, this common card, and all cards of its rank, are wild. (A subtle variation of spit includes the common card but the rank is *not* wild. Just a slight change, but the whole game is different!)

Spit with the common card designating the rank of wild cards is like deuces wild (see Chapter Seven), the rank of wild cards selected arbitrarily, with the difference that everyone has (at least) one wild card. You can play this much as you would deuces wild, except that possession of an "extra" wild card becomes more important and you must readjust your thinking about hand values. Since everyone has a wild card to start with, the average winning hand increases from three kings or three aces (in deuces wild) to about four nines. Thus, full houses are often worthless. If, for example, your four cards are a high pair and a low pair, it is usually better to throw away the low pair than to keep it.

Just to show you how tricky the analysis of these games can be, let's look at the "subtle variation" mentioned above. When the common card and others of its rank are *not* wild, the entire complexion of the game is changed. Now the hands will run considerably *lower* than those in ordinary draw poker—for everyone is "stuck" with the common card in the center and cannot exchange it for a new one in the draw! In this game, a pair of aces is an excellent hand and worth a raise before the draw.

ANACONDA

This game is very popular with the younger set. Probably more college students have lost money at this game than at any other. (But not *as much* money as at other games, for anaconda is rarely played for big stakes.) This is understandable, for it is quite a difficult game and involves several ideas which are found in few other poker games. For this reason, I classify it in the "not recommended" category.

I include a description here because it is the most popular of those dealer's choice games which are not simply jazzed-up variations of the basic games of draw and stud.

Each player is dealt seven cards, face down. No further cards are dealt. After a round of betting* (as in draw poker), each player passes three cards to the player on his left (some groups pass to the right on alternate deals). Each player now discards two cards, face down, leaving himself with a five-card poker hand. He then stacks his five cards one on top of another, face down, *in the order he wishes to expose them in a deal of five-card stud.* This order may not be changed once it has been selected. Each player turns a card and there is a round of betting, following the rules of five-card stud. From this point, the rules of five-card stud are followed except that the successive upcards are turned from the top of each player's pile rather than dealt from the pack. The showdown occurs when each player turns over his last hidden card. Most frequently, the player with the highest-valued poker hand wins the pot; on occasion, high-low is played.

Degrees of skill vary wildly in anaconda. Poor players will stay in too long and bluff too often at the end. In an expert game (high only), I would expect the average winning hand to be queens full, but I can't back up this view with any statistics, since serious players seldom indulge in what they consider a "prep school activity."

Nonetheless, the opportunity for skillful play in anaconda is very great. Here is one tip. In determining your pass, forget about anything less than a full house. Don't try for straights or flushes. Furthermore, the rank of your full house may be crucial. Drop a low full house early if the betting is strong.

* This betting round is sometimes omitted.

Dealer's Choice

GENERAL ADVICE ON UNUSUAL GAMES

If you have any interest in this chapter as a playing guide, it is probable that you are occasionally called upon to play dealer's choice in which all sorts of unusual games are called. You either don't want to look foolish or want to demonstrate your superior poker ability by beating your opponents at their own games. Therefore, I will conclude this chapter with some general advice on unusual games.

1 (and also 2 and 3). Be conservative. "Funny" games are usually played very loosely because no one understands the guiding principles of the game—small wonder, as there are so many different variations. Most of these games involve a large number of betting rounds and juicy pots. By going out early when you don't have sound values, you are assured of being a big winner simply by taking your fair share of the pots on your good hands. Don't speculate. All doubtful situations should be resolved in favor of dropping out.

4. Watch out for situations near the end of a hand in which the pot offers huge odds. Even if you think you are beaten, the pot may offer good enough odds for you to call at the end. (Of course, if you follow 1, 2, and 3, you will not get into many of these situations.)

5. In games with wild cards, don't be influenced by the fact that your hand would be a good one if there were no wild cards. Judge each hand on its poker value *within the game being played.*

6. In loose games, where most people stay in on the early rounds and raises get called on speculation, don't worry too much about driving people out of the pot. Up the stakes when you are clearly ahead. Also, under these conditions, position is not as important as it is in a conservative game.

◎ ◎ ◎ ◎ ◎

ELEVEN

Other Forms of
Betting

This book has been written from the viewpoint of limit betting, that is, a fixed limit on the amount one may bet or raise. There are other forms of betting which sometimes lead to more exciting play—and also to higher stakes. These are generally preferred by gamblers, serious players, experts, and, alas, some inexperienced players who do not know better. You should stay away from these forms of betting until you feel confident that you have mastered everything in this book and have gained a considerable amount of poker experience to back up your knowledge. At that point, you may or may not become interested in the more complicated betting methods. For those of you who will become interested, this chapter will introduce you to the mechanics of **pot limit, table stakes,** and combinations thereof. (I hasten to include my usual warning—you will need more than a description of the mechanics in order to play poker successfully under these conditions.)

Other Forms of Betting

Pot limit betting means just what it says. The amount that one may bet or raise is determined by *the amount in the pot at the time* rather than by a fixed limit. This is the legal *maximum;* one may bet or raise a lesser amount if desired.

For example, in our typical eight-handed game of draw poker, the total ante is $2. The maximum opening bet, therefore, is $2. Suppose that Al opens for $2, Bob calls, and the others drop. There is now $6 in the pot, so after the draw, the maximum opening bet will be $6. It will be observed that these limits are rather higher than the ones usually associated with this poker group. In general, pot-limit betting will be higher than fixed-limit betting by a considerable margin. Since pot-limit betting can get out of hand, it is advisable to have some restriction on it: either a maximum number of raises per round (usually three), or, more in keeping with the spirit of pot limit, a maximum amount that a player may wager in any one pot (500 times the total ante is the average limit of this form).

One tricky feature of pot limit is the amount one is allowed to *raise*. Recall that the raise is based on the amount in the pot *at the time of the raise,* and it is presumed that the player first calls the opposing bet and then raises. Thus, in our sample game, with a $2 total ante, Al opens for $2. If Bob wants to raise, he first puts in $2 to call. He may now raise as much as $6—the *new* amount of the pot. Thus, when there is a raise in pot limit, the amounts can really soar. Here is another example:

Ante $2. Al opens for $2; Bob calls; Charlie raises, putting in a total of $10 ($2 call, $8 raise—the new amount in the pot after his call). Dick, Ed, Frank, George, and Harry all fold. If Al wants to reraise, he may put in $32! ($8 to call

Charlie's raise, $24, the new amount in the pot, to raise.)
And so on.

No doubt you have noticed that pot limit can be *very*
expensive.

TABLE STAKES

Another fairly popular form of betting is table stakes. This
method requires that each player place before him the maximum amount he is willing to wager on the current deal
(his stake). This amount may not be changed during the
deal. Each player's stake is his total betting limit for the
deal. A player may bet or raise any or all of his (remaining)
stake. Similarly, no one can be forced to put *more* than his
stake into the pot in order to reach a showdown. Thus, if Al
and Bob are the last two players remaining, and Al has $50
and Bob has $40, Al may not bet more than $40, the amount
that Bob can call. (If Al inadvertently bets more than $40,
perhaps through not realizing that Bob has only that little,
he may withdraw the excess when Bob announces that his
remaining stake is only $40.) When a player has bet all his
chips, he is said to be tapped. A bet of all one's remaining
chips, or a bet which will cause another player to use all his
chips if he wishes to call, is similarly called a tap.

The use of table stakes can cause some complications.
For example, suppose Al, Bob, and Charlie are contesting
the pot. Al has $50, Bob has $30, and Charlie has $40. Al
wishes to bet the maximum. He may bet $40, since Charlie
is capable of calling that amount. Now suppose that Bob
wants to call. He has a right to reach a showdown by
putting in his remaining $30, even though Al has bet more
than that. So Bob calls $30 worth of Al's bet. The remaining
$10 of Al's bet is a challenge to Charlie but does not affect

Other Forms of Betting

Bob. (Bob cannot win that $10, even if he wins the pot, because he did not put up a comparable amount.) If Charlie wishes to stay in, he must call the entire $40 of Al's bet. Since Bob called for only $30, he has no interest in the extra $10 bet by Al and Charlie. Therefore, this excess $20 goes into a **side pot.** A side pot is a separate pot which does not involve all the players who are still active. The portion of the pot involving all the active players is called the **main pot** or the **center pot.**

The side pot is a contest among those players who have placed bets in it. In the example above, the better hand between Al's and Charlie's entitles its owner to take the side pot ($20 total) while the player with the best hand among Al, Bob, and Charlie will win the main pot. Notice that Al or Charlie may win the side pot and still lose the main pot (if Bob has the best hand of all).

Once a player drops from the pot, he loses his interest in all side pots. Suppose that in the above example, there was another player, Dick, with $100. He raises, putting $30 into the main pot, $10 into the side pot, and bets an additional $10 against what Al still holds. If Al is not willing to call this additional $10, he must drop out of *all* pots. The main pot then would be among Bob, Charlie, and Dick, the side pot between Charlie and Dick. On the other hand, if Al did call this $10 bet, it would create a *second* side pot—one involving only Al and Dick.

This betting and the side pots created (assuming Al called Dick's raise) are summarized in the following table.

WIN AT POKER

SIDE POTS

PLAYERS	AL	BOB	CHARLIE	DICK
Original stake	$50	$30	$40	$100
Main pot ($120; Al, Bob, Charlie and Dick)	Bet $30 (a)	Call $30 (b)	Call $30 (c)	Call $30 (d)
First side pot ($30; Al, Charlie and Dick)	Bet $10 (a)	(Tapped)	Call $10 (c)	Call $10 (d)
Second side pot ($20; Al and Dick)	Call $10 (e)		(Tapped)	Raise $10 (d)

(a) Al bets $40.
   (With Dick in the example, Al could bet his entire $50 at once if he so chose.) $10 of Al's bet goes to the first side pot since Bob has only $30 with which to call.
(b) Bob calls Al's bet, in the main pot, but cannot call in the side pot.
(c) Charlie calls Al's entire bet.
(d) Dick raises Al $10, necessitating a second side pot since Charlie is now tapped.
(e) Al calls the raise.

POT LIMIT-TABLE STAKES

Some poker groups like the idea of table stakes but dislike allowing the possibility of somebody throwing in a huge bet at whim. It's annoying to have some wise guy bet $200 when there is only $5 in the pot, whether or not it is good tactics on his part. These groups combine the ideas behind pot limit and table stakes and restrict bets by *both* the amount in the pot and the amount each player has on the table. In other words, pot-limit rules apply, but no player may bet (or be required to call) more than he has on the table. (When side pots arise, the betting limit in the side pot is governed by the total amount in all pots.)

If and when you become interested in these forms of betting, I suggest you try pot limit-table stakes. It's my personal favorite.

COMMENT ON BETTING LIMITS

The introduction of any of the betting limits described in this chapter has a profound effect on strategy. To make a long story short, you must throw everything except basic principles out the window and relearn each game. The possibility of a raise the size of the pot (or more) at any time makes some types of hand more valuable than others, even though they rank lower. Money management is more difficult and proper technique often depends on the relative size of your stake with those of the other players. Pot limit and table stakes are games for experienced players (only). If your group is used to limit betting and wants to experiment with the other forms, I suggest using pennies or even lower-valued chips for your experiments. Make sure the stakes do not get out of hand during your first attempts, for these forms are in a different world from fixed limits.

TWELVE

◎ ◎ ◎ ◎ ◎

Your Poker Career

In the last few chapters, you have been introduced to more difficult poker games and advanced forms of betting. This material gives you a good idea of the directions in which you should expand your technical knowledge should you decide to continue your career as a poker player.

In this, my final chapter, I will indicate the directions in which you should expand your thinking about the game, so that your poker maturity can keep pace with your ever-growing knowledge of new poker forms. Also, I include a few odds and ends which may be valuable to you: remarks on how to set up your own poker game; a summary of my suggested rules for more enjoyable poker; a checklist of things to remember when you play in a strange game; a recapitulation of the highlights of winning strategy; and a list of the order in which you should attempt to learn the different forms of poker.

Throughout this book I have scattered warnings to proceed with your poker learning at a leisurely rate—not to advance from chapter to chapter or one form of poker to another until you feel confidence in what you have learned to that point. This will be my final warning. Although I present an outline for your future poker development, it is not intended to be a "next step" but rather an overall description of a long process. Take your time. The fable doesn't mention it, but the tortoise was a winner at the poker table; the hare was not.

IMPROVING YOUR PLAY

In each form of poker you play, improvement will depend largely on poker analysis. This means that you must be able to determine the nature of your opponents' hands from their betting habits (or, in rare cases, from mannerisms). Much of this is a matter of remembering how the players in your game behaved on previous occasions. Just as baseball pitchers keep a "book" on every batter, and therefore know what pitches are likely to be most effective against them, so you should keep track of the habits of the "batters" in your game and thus determine the best way to beat them.

Knowledge of opponents' habits is the surest guide at closed (draw) poker, in which you do not see any cards other than your own. However, at open (stud) poker, you have more information available. Because portions of each player's hand are exposed, you can count the cards. Also, you can draw inferences about the nature of the concealed (hole) cards of the other players.

My recommendation on counting cards was to begin by remembering cards you were looking for. The next stage is to count all the *crucial* cards: in high games, the cards of interest to you and your opponents; in low games, all the low cards (seven or lower). The final stage in your counting process is to count many (or, if you are especially talented, *all*) cards. This will be a considerable strain at first, but there is a just reward awaiting you when you have reached this degree of skill: when you are able to count cards, you will find yourself remembering only those which are of significance. Thus, after a lot of hard work struggling to learn to count, it will no longer require any conscious thought, and you will be free to think about other things.

After you are able to count the cards you can *see,* you must then start counting cards which you did not see, but which you can identify from the progress of the game. Here are two examples of counting hidden cards. Recall Bob, our conservative player. Let's watch Bob play two hands and determine (for counting purposes) what his hidden hole card was.

First, five-card high stud. Bob stays on the first round with a seven for his upcard when there were two kings on board. On the next round, he receives an ace for an upcard and drops in the face of a bet from an open pair. Bob's hole card was a seven. He would not have stayed on the first round without a seven or an ace in the hole (a king might normally be a possibility but not when there were two others showing) and it is now obvious that he did not have an ace.

Second example, five-card (or six-card) low stud. Bob stays on the first round with a five for his upcard, stays on the second round with a three for his second upcard, but then drops on the next round when he receives a four for his third upcard. Clearly his hole card is a four. Why else would he have liked his hand up to now and suddenly decide to drop when he receives what seems to be a good card?

These examples are elementary but illustrate the type of thinking which will enable you to count more cards than the ones that are exposed to view. Sometimes you will need to know a player's tendencies in order to determine (or make an intelligent guess at) his hole card. For example, if Bob were a loose first-round caller, it would not be a certainty that he had a seven in the hole in the first example;

perhaps he would play with a queen. The highest level of counting skill combines poker knowledge with extra information based on the habits of your opponents.

As you become a more experienced player, you will be able to notice more than the minimum necessary to keep your head above water. For example, some players have mannerisms which tip off the nature of their hands; others will act in different ways depending on their results during the session (many players bluff near the end of a session in a desperate attempt to get even). Similarly, you will be able to give equal concentration to the important task of avoiding such tipoffs about your own hand. "Keep a poker face" is an expression implying that a successful poker player should remain devoid of expression at all times, presumably presenting nothing more than a stony glare to his opponents' searching eyes. I have found such extreme measures to be unnecessary, but nonetheless you should examine your own behavior in situations in which you expect to win, hope to win, are worried, are bluffing, and so on, to make sure there is no telltale pattern to your actions. Not allowing your opponents to gain information from your demeanor is just as important as not letting them detect an unvarying pattern in your strategy.

A final note along these lines may be worth montion. You may find that there is a player who "has your number" in that he seems always (or almost always) to make the right decision when he opposes you in a pot. This is not luck—you are either giving your hand away or being outplayed. If you cannot determine anything you are doing which might be tipping off your nemesis, your best course is to avoid becoming involved with this player (by waiting for sounder than usual values to enter a pot against him, etc.) or, in emergencies (where *all* your opponents beat you), to find weaker compctition.

WIN AT POKER

Suppose you are interested in beginning your own poker group or in improving the games in which your present group participates. What are the important matters that require discussion and agreement? As far as specific rules are concerned, in the next section I will summarize the suggestions I have made throughout this book. Also my recommendations for dealing with irregularities will be found in the appendix. Here is a list of other considerations and some suggestions for dealing with them:

1. *Setting the rules.*

Once you have determined the rules which will govern your game, *write them down.* A list of all agreements and understandings should be present where the game is played; if possible, each player should be given a copy. This procedure can be simplified by agreeing to use the rules in this or some other book, possibly with a few modifications to suit the tastes of the individual players. If a book is used as an official reference, this should also be specified in the written rules.

The objective of writing down the rules is to avoid arguments. If a disagreement arises, many or all of the players may have a financial interest in the outcome. Further, it is unpleasant to be placed in the position of being forced to arbitrate where whatever you say will make you unpopular with at least one person. If you have a written rule covering the area of disagreement, there is no room for argument. It therefore follows that the written rules should be made as complete as possible.

2. *Money, chips and stakes.*

Rules for settling the game (I suggest that all accounts be settled after the session, in any event before the next session), the method of buying and selling chips (simplest is for the host to act as a banker and both sell and redeem all chips), and possible variation in the stakes are essential.

Poker lacks some of its charm (for me, anyway) when someone loses more than he can afford. Therefore, when the matter of stakes is discussed, I recommend that each player be forced to set his own personal limit for the maximum amount he is willing to lose during the session and *not be allowed to buy chips above that limit.* Most people are able to set sensible limits before the game begins, but lose sight of reality when losing heavily. The advance-limit technique will avoid a disastrous loss and thereby keep the game friendly.

Similarly, I recommend that the established betting limits be maintained. Most games tend to raise the stakes during a session (usually at the urging of the losers, who then lose at a higher rate) or for the last round. I disapprove of this as being conducive to loose play and causing additional and unnecessary losses to the players who are already losing. Only in purely social, low-stake games, should such deviations be tolerated.

3. *Players.*

Most poker games are "closed" in that they are restricted to a group of players which remains constant (although not all may show up for a particular session). Others, however, allow friends of the regular players into the game; some abide complete strangers.

Whatever the philosophy of your poker group in this regard, it should be a part of the written rules. Here I have no recommendation.

4. *Time.*

Time limits should be established and adhered to strictly. Poker games tend to drag on, again on the incentive of the losers. I suggest establishing a fixed time for ending the game and sticking to it without exception. If you allow the time for ending the game to remain uncertain, you will eventually discover yourself playing all night, or, at the very least, later than you really want to. (I know, because it has happened to me. Even extra winnings won't make up for the way you feel the next morning.)

It is equally important to get the game *started* on time, for late starts are bound to increase the desire of the players to exceed the established time for stopping. Emphasize to all those involved that the game starts on time. In fact, schedule the game for ten or fifteen minutes *before* you want to begin, and actually start playing at that time, even though several players are missing. This will foster the impression that no one will have to wait around if he comes on time. Nothing will do more to cause tardiness than being unable to start at the announced starting time. Players will arrive on time and find they have to cool their heels for a half hour. Next time, they will come half an hour later, leading to a degeneration of the established starting time.

The matter of time limits may seem a trivial one, but my experience is that sticking to established time limits on both ends is the most important factor in keeping a poker group together. (The only contender for the honor is that the big losers run out of money.)

SUMMARY OF SUGGESTED RULES

For your ready reference in discussions with your poker friends, here is a list of my suggested rules. Remember that it is important to *write down* which rules your group has adopted.

TOPIC	SUGGESTED RULE
Ante	Have each dealer ante "for the game."
Split openers	In jackpots, *always* place opener's discards face down in the pot.
Choice of games	Inexperienced players should stick to the basic games; each player in turn should be allowed to select the game to be played for a full round (otherwise, a buck must be used for draw poker). Two players' objections to a game should constitute a veto.
Betting limits	Inexperienced players should use fixed-limit betting; if a limit on the number of raises per round is desired, use a limit of a *total* of three raises (by anyone) per round.
Check-and-raise (sandbagging)	Should be allowed.
Coffeehousing and conversation	Should be allowed, but not to the extent that it will be annoying, or disturb the concentration of any player, or delay the game.
Games involving low hands	Aces, straights, and flushes should be considered as either high or low at the holder's option.
Low stud	Player with *lowest* board should act first in each betting round.
Stud poker	Designated player should be required to bet or drop in first betting round.
Irregularities	As recommended in the appendix.

CHECKLIST FOR PLAYING IN A STRANGE GAME

It is always highly desirable to watch any poker game before you play in it. Should this prove impossible, the most important points to check on before playing are the following:

1. Rules, especially the topics listed in the previous section and in the appendix.

2. Etiquette, especially what you may say or do without being considered unethical (or worse) and becoming unpopular.

3. Local variations. Many poker groups employ special rules, even special poker hands, which are not standard. Be sure to inquire in this direction before playing.

A SUMMARY OF POKER STRATEGY

For those nervous moments before the game begins, here is a capsule summary of the highlights of the advice given in this book. If, on reading it through at the present time, you do not recall the significance of any item, I suggest you return to the appropriate chapter for a second reading.

TOPIC	HIGHLIGHTS
How to learn	Read; observe; play.
	Watch a game before you join it.
Basic principles	Money management—set limits before playing.
	Principle of betting—compare chance to win with odds offered by the pot.
	Mathematics—know hand values;

TOPIC	HIGHLIGHTS
	know basic odds against improving; a raise shortens the pot odds.
	Poker overhead—compare the ante with the betting limit.
	Position—in draw, depends on location of dealer or opener; in stud, depends on location of man with high board.
	Psychology—don't overdo your bluffing.
Draw poker	Before the draw: know your values; position is very important.
	The draw: change the standard draw only for deception or to try to beat a specific hand.
	After the draw: personalities are paramount.
Stud poker	Be very conservative.
	Don't play if you can't beat the board.
Games with extra cards	Get out early, as soon as you get a bad card in most cases.
Wild cards	It is better to have wild cards than natural cards.
	Adjust hand values.
Dealer's choice games	Be ultraconservative in a new game.

WIN AT POKER

Here is a summary of the different poker games, grouped with a view toward indicating when it is suitable for you to start learning, watching, and eventually playing each. Within each group, the games are listed in the recommended order of learning.

Can be played based on advice in this book	Suitable for beginners	Draw poker Jackpots Five-card stud
	Require some poker experience	Draw poker with wild cards Baseball Spit in the ocean
Should not be played seriously without further reading	Depend on basic principles	Seven-card stud Low stud
	May require specialized knowledge	Other "dealer's choice" games, excluding high-low and special (not draw or stud) games such as anaconda. Lowball
Not recommended; should not be played without considerable study and experience		Anaconda and similar games High-low (all forms)

Your Poker Career

If you become a serious poker player you will want two further pieces of information : (1) what books are available on more advanced strategy and (2) where you can turn for poker advice on topics which cannot be located in any published work.

(1) Books.

Although there have been a considerable number of books published on poker, the literature is more limited than that of other popular games. In fact, I wrote this book because I felt there was a need for a basic text for beginners and inexperienced players. (If you are a beginning contract bridge or chess player, you have a problem deciding which elementary manual to follow; if you are a beginning poker player, you have trouble finding *anything* that will help you.)

For the advancing player, however, the bookshelves of stores and libraries hold more promise. On the intermediate level, and as an introduction to advanced strategy, I recommend *Poker* by Oswald Jacoby. Those interested in complete details on play at all levels (including expert tactics) should read *The Complete Guide to Winning Poker* by Albert H. Morehead.

(2) Advice and answers.

If you find yourself in need of poker advice, or have a question on any phase of the game (laws, ethics, strategy, etc.), and assuming you find the advice in this book satisfactory, you may send your query to me and I will be happy to answer it.

WIN AT POKER

Please include a stamped, self-addressed envelope with your question, and send it to me at

The Bridge World
39 West 94th St.
New York, N.Y. 10025

◎ ◎ ◎ ◎ ◎

The Modern Laws
of Poker

As advertised (in Chapter One), this appendix presents laws of poker which apply to irregularities. For each situation, I give the traditional law, my recommendation (whether or not to change it, and if so how) which is usually the modern treatment, and comment on the reason(s) behind my suggestion. I sincerely hope you will give some thought to these ideas, for I believe that poker will never gain the status and recognition it deserves until a sound code of laws is universally adopted.

1. Redeals.

Traditional:

(a) Any player may require a redeal before a stated time limit if:

> (i) a card was exposed in shuffling or cutting;
>
> (ii) one packet of the cut contained four or fewer cards;
>
> (iii) two or more cards are faced in the pack;

   (iv) the pack contains too few cards, too many
        cards, any card or cards distinguishable by
        markings or other means, or duplicated cards;
   (v) a player is dealing out of turn.

(b) No player may require a redeal if he has looked at any of his own cards.

(c) If a redeal is required, the deal reverts to the proper dealer, regardless of who was dealing when the redeal was called.

(d) If an incorrect dealer is discovered after a bet has been made, such bet or bets are forfeited to the pot and the proper dealer deals. However, no player need ante for the redeal. This rule is waived, and a deal out of turn stands, if no redeal is called before the stated time limit elapses.

Recommendation:

Omit (a) (i). Instead, add: "If any player has seen any card that card is reshuffled with the undealt portion of the pack."

Comment: However the card became exposed, knowing a card can give a player an advantage, even though it might be negligible on any one deal.

Recommendation: Omit (a) (ii).

Comment: This rule is meaningless and may cause confusion when a short pack (required by a reshuffle of discards, see page 33) is being dealt.

Recommendation: Omit (a) (iii).

Comment: Faced cards should simply be reshuffled.

Recommendation : Retain (a) (iv).

Comment: In theory, if the pack was imperfect, the deal was improper to begin with.

Recommendation: Omit (a) (v).

Comment: It is no tragedy if a player deals out of turn. The deal can be completed, the next deal revert to the proper dealer, and the improper dealer skipped the next time the deal reaches him. The only exception is at jack-pots, when the amount of the ante may vary from deal to deal. In this case, an improper dealer should be equivalent to an imperfect pack.

Recommendation: Change the "stated time limit" in (a) to "before any action has been taken in the first betting round or any upcard has been exposed."

Comment: The time limit is traditionally before the second round of cards is dealt. Since only betting action or exposed cards give anyone information about the deal, the suggested time is superior.

Recommendation: Omit (b); retain (c).

Comment: A redeal should be called only if there is no other way to adjust the situation; there is no reason not to have the proper player deal the redeal.

Recommendation: Substitute for (d): "If a redeal is required after any bets have been made, such bets may be withdrawn from the pot."

Comment: A player who bet may in no way be responsible for causing the redeal, and should not be required to know who the proper dealer was. Also, the traditional rule allows waiting for a bet to be made before (properly) calling for a redeal and thus encourages "sharp" practices. As a general rule, redeals should occur only when the pack is imperfect or some completely unforeseeable situation arises. Exposed cards, which can be reshuffled, should not be cause for a redeal.

2. Misdeals.

Traditional:

(a) If there is a misdeal owing to dealer's error, the dealer forfeits the right to deal and to any ante made solely by him.

(b) A misdeal may be called by a player who has not

intentionally seen any of his cards, if done so prior to . . .
(various rules depending on the nature of the game).

(c) If not enough cards are dealt, the deal must be completed.

(d) If not enough hands are dealt, dealer gives his own hand to the first player to his left missing a hand. Others missing hands may withdraw their antes.

(e) If too many hands are dealt, one of them is declared dead and that hand discarded. No hand may be declared dead if a player has seen a card in that hand.

Recommendation: Replace (a) with: "If there is a misdeal, no matter what the cause, the deal is repeated with no penalty."

Comment: Poker is not intended as a dealing contest.

Recommendation: In (b), the time limit should be as recommended in 1 (a).

Comment: The same considerations apply.

Recommendation: Retain (c). Replace (d) with: "If not enough hands are dealt, the deal is completed." Retain (e).

Comment: There is no objection, for example, if a missing hand in draw poker is completed with five consecutive cards. Notice that in (e) no hand with a faced upcard may be discarded and thus the situation may call for an application of the exposed card rule (see below).

3. Incorrect hand.

Traditional:

If a hand has more or fewer than the designated number of cards, it is foul and cannot win the pot.

Recommendation: Omit "or fewer."

Comment: No one has been jeopardized, except the holder of the hand, if a player is missing a card. If someone can win with four cards when others have five, more power to him.

4. Betting irregularities.

Traditional:

No chips may be withdrawn from the pot except by a player who has been dealt out, failed to receive the proper number of hole cards at stud poker, or bet after another opened without the requirements (at jackpots).

Recommendation: Add: "but any chips placed in the pot in error may be removed."

Comment: Once again, there are certain things poker is not designed to test. If a player puts in $3 while announcing he is calling a $2 bet, he should be allowed to take back his extra dollar. This should also apply to bets above the limit and similar errors. "Muggins" is for cribbage players.

5. Announcements of intentions; actions out of turn.

Traditional: Too complicated to bear listing.

Recommendation: Any announcement in turn is equivalent to taking that action; any announcement out of turn is meaningless; any action (bet, call, raise, drop, etc.) out of turn is also meaningless.

Comment: Of course, no one should take any *action* out of turn. However, penalties are generally ineffective and may lead to hard feeling. Social pressure is the best way to avoid recurrences.

Whether out-of-turn *announcements* ("if you bet, I'll raise" and so on) are allowed depends on the spirit of the game. In any event, my recommendation is simple and should avoid arguments.

6. Exposed cards.

Traditional:

(a) Each player is responsible for his own hand. If he exposes one of his own cards, or allows another player to expose one, he has no redress.

(b) A card exposed in the pack after the deal is dead and is placed among the discards.

(c) A card exposed during the deal must be dealt to the player to whom it was intended.

Recommendation: Replace these rules with: "An exposed card should be replaced in the pack and the pack be reshuffled before the deal continues."

Comment: It is grossly unfair to give a player an exposed card. Similarly, there is no reason to take the card out of the deck, which may cause even more harm than the knowledge that this card is not one of the concealed cards.

7. The showdown.

Traditional:

(a) If a player has misstated his hand, his values may be restated until such time as the amount that was in the pot can no longer be determined.

(b) Concessions may be corrected until the time period described in (a).

Recommendation: Retain these rules.

Comment: It should be the policy of the game to correct errors. Thus, if a pot is appropriated in error, and the error is discovered, the game should agree that an attempt be made to reconstruct the amount that was in the pot and award it to its rightful owner. Poker may be a bloodthirsty game, but it is also a gentleman's game.

8. Special rules.

Traditional:

(a) If a player opens at jackpots without the proper values, his hand is void.

(b) If a player makes an impossible call, he may withdraw his bet.

Recommendation: Retain these rules.

Comment: An example of (b), the so-called "idiot's rule," would be as follows. At five-card stud poker, Al has

Hole card	♣ Q			
Upcards:	♦ 10	♥ Q	♥ 8	♣ A

Bob, his opponent, bets with these upcards:

♠ K   ♦ 4   ♥ 10   ♣ K

A call by Al would be "impossible" since he cannot beat the board and it is time for a showdown. (A raise, however, would *not* be impossible, since it does not force a showdown, and Al has a possible bluff, representing a pair of aces.)

REMARKS ON RULES

Whether you agree or disagree with my suggested rules—those presented in this appendix for dealing with irregularities or those elsewhere in the book—it is essential for your poker group to have a *written* code of rules. For purposes of keeping peace in your poker game, any *written* set of rules will suffice. *But you must have a set to follow.* Further, any additional special rules which your group wishes to enforce (such special rules are called house rules) should also be written and made known to all players. Some of the topics you may want to cover in the house rules are listed in Chapter Twelve under "How to Run a Poker Game." There may also be others you will wish to include.

Every now and then there may be an argument which is not covered by any rule you have, or there may be an ambiguity discovered in one of your existing rules. When this occurs, settle the argument as fairly and amicably as possible (I recommend "equity over law" in cases of ambiguity), *immediately* decide your future policy in the matter, and *immediately* WRITE it into the house rules.

With money, personalities, and egos involved in poker as much as they are, there are bound to be unpleasant clashes unless written rules are available to act as judge and jury. This is one of poker's major problems, and every poker player has an obligation to improve the game and make it more enjoyable by eliminating potential sources of friction.

GLOSSARY AND INDEX

In order to make this book useful as a reference I have combined the glossary and index. All important terms used in the book are included as well as a few other common terms, taken from popular poker jargon, which you may hear at a poker game and not understand. I have differentiated "poker slang"—as it might irreverently be called—by designating poker language with the symbol (P) to distinguish it from the technical language.

Each term, phrase, title or whatever is followed by a definition; a boldface page number indicates where it or a synonym first appears in the book, and, on occasion, additional page numbers indicate where special attention is given to the topic.

the deal; to put in such chips. 18

Back-to-back (P)
hole card and first upcard forming a pair at five-card stud. 104

Baseball
a dealer's choice stud game in which threes and nines are wild, involving extra cards and special betting rules. 169, 179

Beans (P)
chips.

Beat the board
have a higher poker combination than the upcards of any other player. 105

Bet
chips put in the pot; to put chips in the pot; the first wager in a betting interval. 15

Bet blind
bet without looking at one's cards. 42

Betting interval
period during which each active player in turn has the right to check, bet, raise, or drop. 13

Bicycle
the lowest possible hand (when aces may be low): 5–4–3–2–A; wheel. 11

Blind (P)
without looking at one's cards. 42

Blind and Straddle
a form of draw poker involving blind openings and raises. 41

Bluff
bet on a hand not expected to be the best. 21, 75

Bluffing
pretending to hold a better hand than one does, usually by betting strongly, in the hope that all others will drop from the pot. 21, 75, 133

Board
in stud poker, an active player's upcards. 105

Boost (P)
raise.

Boys (P)
jacks.

Buck
a token used to signify the next player assuming the rights of the dealer in draw poker. 176

Bug
a wild card restricted to use as an ace or a card to fill a flush or straight at high poker; equivalent to a joker at low poker. 146

Bull (P)
ace.

Bullet (P)
ace.

Bump (P)
raise.

Bust (P)
fail to draw successfully; a poor hand; receive a picture card or pairing card at low poker.

Buy (P)
draw.

Call
put chips in the pot to match another's bet. 16

Cards speak
at high-low, a showdown procedure in which the players need not declare an intention to try for any specified portion of the pot but simply expose their cards as in high poker. 167

Case card (P)
the last unseen card of a rank or a suit.

Center pot
  pot in which all active players have an interest (as opposed to a side pot). 187
Check
  denial of the desire to bet which does not forfeit rights to remain active. 15
Check-and-raise
  checking and then raising in the same betting interval. 21
Checked out
  (of a betting round) completed with no bet being made; (of a deal) at draw poker, completed with no opening bet, and therefore ended. 16
Chip
  a token used instead of money. 194
Cinch hand (P)
  hand sure to win the pot.
Closed poker
  the form of poker in which no cards are exposed until the showdown. 99
Close to the belly (P)
  conservative betting; cards held so that no opponent can see their faces.
Close to the chest (P)
  conservatively.
Coffee-housing
  attempting to confuse or mislead opponents through speech and manner. 20
Common card
  a card part of each player's hand. 160
Concealed pair
  a pair entirely contained among a player's hole cards. 131
Consecutive declaration
  at high-low, a showdown procedure in which the active players indicate their declara-

tions in a specified order. 168
Cowboys (P)
  kings.
Crazy (P)
  wild.
Cut
  divide the pack into two parts. 36

Dame (P)
  queen.
Deal
  distribute cards to the players; the time period of such distribution; the time period from the distribution of cards to the showdown. 13
Dealer's choice
  rule allowing the dealer to determine the form of poker to be played; an unusual game. 169, 175, 183
Deck
  pack. 8
Declaration
  in high-low poker, an indication that one is trying for high, low, or both. 168
Deuce
  two-spot. 8
Deuces-wild
  draw poker in which deuces are wild cards. 146
Discards
  throws away; all the abandoned cards. 33
Downcard
  hole card; card dealt facedown. 99
Down the river (P)
  seven-card stud.
Draw
  receive cards to replace discards. 28, 32, 86
Draw dealer
  in dealer's choice, the player designated as having the rights and obligations of the

dealer in draw poker, regardless of which player actually dealt the cards. 176

Draw poker
closed poker in which the active players discard and receive new cards. 28, 30, 81

Drop
withdraw from the pot. 13

Duffer (P)
unskillful player.

Eldest hand
player nearest the dealer's left; age. 32

Exposed
face up. 99

Exposed pair
open pair. 101

Face card
any king, queen, or jack.

Faced
lying face up; exposed. 99

Fever (P)
a five-spot.

Fill (P)
draw or receive a favorable card; make a good hand through improvement of previous values.

First jack deals
a popular method of selecting the original dealer: cards are dealt face up in rotation, and the player receiving the first jack deals.

First hand
the first player in turn. 32

Five-of-a-kind
the highest-ranking hand, composed of five cards of the same rank (possible only in wild-card games). 145

Fixed limit
betting limit which states the maximum amount a player may bet or raise. 17

Flush
five cards of the same suit. 10

Fold (P)
drop. 107

Four-flush
four cards of the same suit. 65

Four-of-a-kind
four cards of the same rank. 9

Fours (P)
four-of-a-kind.

Freak (P)
wild card.

Freak-pots (P)
Deuces wild.

Free ride (P)
a betting interval (except the last) in which everyone checks.

Full hand (P)
full house.

Full house
three cards of one rank and two cards of another. 10

Game
form of poker; (P) poker group; collection of players.

Girls (P)
queens.

Go out
drop. 13

Hand
cards held by a player. 8

High
highest-ranking; poker form in which player with highest-ranking hand in the showdown wins the pot. 166

High
headed by the card named, as "king-high" (having a king as its highest card). 12

High-low
a form of poker in which

half the pot is awarded to the player with the highest-ranking poker hand and half the pot is awarded to the player with the lowest-ranking poker hand. 165

Hit (P)
fill; draw successfully; be dealt a good card.

Hole card
card dealt face down; down-card. 99

Hookers (P)
queens.

House rules
special rules agreed on by a group of poker players. 22

Hustler (P)
expert who seeks weaker competition.

Immortal
hand sure to win; cinch hand. 122

Impossible call
a call which must, on the face of the exposed cards of other players, lose. 208

Improve
draw or receive cards yielding a superior poker combination to that previously held. 26, 64, 88

In
having called; active (player); having paid an ante. 17

Initial bet
the first bet made in a betting round. 15

Inside straight
four cards in incomplete sequence, e.g., Q-J-9-8. 38

Interval of betting
period during which bets may be made and are equalized. 13

In-the-hole (P)
card(s) dealt face down in stud poker. 104

Irregularity
an unintentional departure from correct procedure. 22, 203

Jackpots
draw poker with a pair of jacks (or better) required to open the betting. 40, 91

J-bird or J-boy (P)
jack.

Johns (P)
jacks.

Joker
an unrestricted wild card added to the deck. 146

Kibitzer (P)
spectator.

Kick (P)
raise.

Kicker
unmatched card held when drawing. 87

Knave (P) (also British)
jack.

Ladies (P)
queens.

Lead (P)
make a voluntary bet.

Limit
the maximum bet or raise allowed. 17

Limit betting
form of betting under which the maximum amount one may bet or raise in turn is a fixed amount. 17

Live (P)
in stud poker, (a card) able or likely to be paired.

Lowball
draw poker in which the lowest-ranking hand wins. 162

Low poker
poker form in which the lowest-ranking hand wins. 158

Main pot
pot involving all active players; the first pot formed in a deal, as opposed to side pots; center pot. 187

Meet (P)
call.

Misdeal
an irregularity in dealing. 205

Money management
management of finances and risks having no direct relation to the laws of poker or strategy. 52

Natural
(card) used in its normal rank and suit; not wild. 147

No pair
poker hand containing no two cards of the same rank or any high-valued poker combination. 12

Odds
a statement of probability as a ratio. 47, 57, 58

One-eyes (P)
face cards showing profiles, thus with only one eye; ♠J, ♥J, ♦K. 146

One pair
hand containing two cards of the same rank. 12

Open
in draw poker, bet originally in the first betting interval; poker form in which some cards are dealt face-up. 99

Open-ended four-straight
four cards in sequence which can be completed to a straight by the addition of a card in sequence at either end, e.g., 9–8–7–6. 38

Opener
player who opens. 34

Openers
the values used by a player to justify opening the pot at jackpots. 41

Open pair
in stud poker, a pair among a player's upcards. 101

Overhead
a poker player's continuing expense for the right to receive cards and place bets in the pot, represented by the ante. 66

Pack
deck. 8

Pair
two cards of the same rank. 11

Palooka (P)
mediocre player.

Pass (P)
check.

Passed-out
a deal or betting round on which no player makes a bet; checked out. 16

Pat
a draw of no cards; hand requiring no draw. 85

Play
call; stay in; betting; action. 16

Player
participant; (P) still active as opposed to having dropped.

Poker
card game in which bets are made on which player has the most valuable five-card combination. 8

Position
relative seating of the players. 69

Pot
accumulation of all antes and bets. 8

Pot limit
limitation of a bet or raise to the amount in the pot. 184, 185

Pot limit-table stakes
a betting rule which limits the amount of a bet or raise both by the amount then in the pot and the stakes of the players. 188

Progressive Jackpots
Jackpots with redealt hands requiring additional opening values. 41

Rabbit (P)
poor player.

Raise
bet more than necessary to call. 16, 65, 84

Rank
position of a card in its suit. 8

Redeal
a new deal caused by an irregularity during dealing. 203

Represent
to bet as though one has a holding other than the actual one; bluff. 21

Reraise
raise following another in the same betting interval. 16, 85

Round
one deal by each participating player. 175

Royal flush
an ace-high straight-flush. 9

Run (P)
straight.

Sandbag
check with a strong hand, hoping to raise later. 21

See (P)
call.

Seven-card stud
stud poker with each player dealt seven cards. 127

Seven-toed Pete (P)
seven-card stud.

Showdown
comparison of the hands of active players to determine the winner. 14

Shuffle
mix the cards. 34

Sidepot
pot separate from the main pot, caused by a tap at table stakes. 187

Sight (P)
final call; right to be in the showdown.

Simultaneous declaration
at high-low, a showdown procedure in which the active players indicate their declarations without knowing how any others have declared. 168

Six-card stud
stud poker in which a player is dealt six cards. 135, 161

Spit-in-the-Ocean
a dealer's choice game involving a common card. 169, 180

Split pair
two cards of the same rank, one among a player's hole cards, the other among his up-cards. 131

Spot card
any card of rank 10,9,8,7, 6,5,4,3, or 2. 8

Stake
the money or chips with which a player enters a game, or (at table stakes) a particular deal. 186

Standard pack
52 cards; 13 of each suit

(spades, hearts, diamonds, clubs); in each suit A,K,Q,J, 10,9,8,7,6,5,4,3,2. 8

Stand pat
    draw no cards. 85

Stay (P)
    call; refuse to drop.

Straddle
    a blind raise of a blind opening, made before the draw at draw poker. 42

Straight
    five cards in sequence. 10

Straight-flush
    five cards of the same suit in sequence. 9

Straight poker
    closed poker with no draw. 41

Stud poker
    form of poker in which some cards are dealt face-up. 99

Suit
    any of the four sets of 13 cards in the standard pack: spades (♠), hearts (♥), diamonds (♦), and clubs (♣). 8

Table (P)
    group of players; upcards; board.

Table stakes
    form of betting limit in which a player may bet as much as he has on the table in front of him, but no more. 184, 186

Tap
    a bet of all one's remaining chips; to make such a bet; to require another player to use all his remaining stake to call. 186

Tapped (P)
    out of chips; having been forced to use all one's remaining chips to call a bet; unable to continue playing through lack of funds. 186

Three of a kind
    a hand containing three cards of one rank and two unmatched cards. 11

Threes (P)
    three-of-a-kind.

Trey
    three-spot. 8

Triplets (P)
    three-of-a-kind. 11

Trips (P)
    triplets; three-of-a-kind.

Two pairs
    pairs of two different ranks. 11

Two-way winner
    at high-low, a hand that wins both the high and low portions of the pot. 175

Under the gun(s) (P)
    in draw poker, the eldest hand.

-up
    two pairs, the higher-ranking being designated, as in "aces-up." 11

Up
    facing; exposed. 99

Upcard
    a card dealt face up. 99

Wheel
    the lowest possible hand: 5–4–3–2–A; bicycle. 11

Whore (P)
    queen.

Wild card
    a card whose holder may designate it as any card. 9, 141

Wired (P)
    back-to-back.

A CATALOG OF SELECTED
DOVER BOOKS
IN ALL FIELDS OF INTEREST

A CATALOG OF SELECTED DOVER
BOOKS IN ALL FIELDS OF INTEREST

DRAWINGS OF REMBRANDT, edited by Seymour Slive. Updated Lippmann, Hofstede de Groot edition, with definitive scholarly apparatus. All portraits, biblical sketches, landscapes, nudes. Oriental figures, classical studies, together with selection of work by followers. 550 illustrations. Total of 630pp. 9⅛ × 12¼.
21485-0, 21486-9 Pa., Two-vol. set $29.90

GHOST AND HORROR STORIES OF AMBROSE BIERCE, Ambrose Bierce. 24 tales vividly imagined, strangely prophetic, and decades ahead of their time in technical skill: "The Damned Thing," "An Inhabitant of Carcosa," "The Eyes of the Panther," "Moxon's Master," and 20 more. 199pp. 5⅜ × 8½. 20767-6 Pa. $4.95

ETHICAL WRITINGS OF MAIMONIDES, Maimonides. Most significant ethical works of great medieval sage, newly translated for utmost precision, readability. Laws Concerning Character Traits, Eight Chapters, more. 192pp. 5⅜ × 8½.
24522-5 Pa. $4.50

THE EXPLORATION OF THE COLORADO RIVER AND ITS CANYONS, J. W. Powell. Full text of Powell's 1,000-mile expedition down the fabled Colorado in 1869. Superb account of terrain, geology, vegetation, Indians, famine, mutiny, treacherous rapids, mighty canyons, during exploration of last unknown part of continental U.S. 400pp. 5⅜ × 8½. 20094-9 Pa. $7.95

HISTORY OF PHILOSOPHY, Julián Marías. Clearest one-volume history on the market. Every major philosopher and dozens of others, to Existentialism and later. 505pp. 5⅜ × 8½. 21739-6 Pa. $9.95

ALL ABOUT LIGHTNING, Martin A. Uman. Highly readable non-technical survey of nature and causes of lightning, thunderstorms, ball lightning, St. Elmo's Fire, much more. Illustrated. 192pp. 5⅜ × 8½. 25237-X Pa. $5.95

SAILING ALONE AROUND THE WORLD, Captain Joshua Slocum. First man to sail around the world, alone, in small boat. One of great feats of seamanship told in delightful manner. 67 illustrations. 294pp. 5⅜ × 8½. 20326-3 Pa. $4.95

LETTERS AND NOTES ON THE MANNERS, CUSTOMS AND CONDITIONS OF THE NORTH AMERICAN INDIANS, George Catlin. Classic account of life among Plains Indians: ceremonies, hunt, warfare, etc. 312 plates. 572pp. of text. 6⅛ × 9¼. 22118-0, 22119-9, Pa. Two-vol. set $17.90

ALASKA: The Harriman Expedition, 1899, John Burroughs, John Muir, et al. Informative, engrossing accounts of two-month, 9,000-mile expedition. Native peoples, wildlife, forests, geography, salmon industry, glaciers, more. Profusely illustrated. 240 black-and-white line drawings. 124 black-and-white photographs. 3 maps. Index. 576pp. 5⅜ × 8½. 25109-8 Pa. $11.95

THE BOOK OF BEASTS: Being a Translation from a Latin Bestiary of the Twelfth Century, T. H. White. Wonderful catalog real and fanciful beasts: manticore, griffin, phoenix, amphivius, jaculus, many more. White's witty erudite commentary on scientific, historical aspects. Fascinating glimpse of medieval mind. Illustrated. 296pp. 5⅜ × 8¼. (Available in U.S. only)   24609-4 Pa. $6.95

FRANK LLOYD WRIGHT: ARCHITECTURE AND NATURE With 160 Illustrations, Donald Hoffmann. Profusely illustrated study of influence of nature—especially prairie—on Wright's designs for Fallingwater, Robie House, Guggenheim Museum, other masterpieces. 96pp. 9¼ × 10¾.   25098-9 Pa. $8.95

FRANK LLOYD WRIGHT'S FALLINGWATER, Donald Hoffmann. Wright's famous waterfall house: planning and construction of organic idea. History of site, owners, Wright's personal involvement. Photographs of various stages of building. Preface by Edgar Kaufmann, Jr. 100 illustrations. 112pp. 9¼ × 10.
       23671-4 Pa. $8.95

YEARS WITH FRANK LLOYD WRIGHT: Apprentice to Genius, Edgar Tafel. Insightful memoir by a former apprentice presents a revealing portrait of Wright the man, the inspired teacher, the greatest American architect. 372 black-and-white illustrations. Preface. Index. vi + 228pp. 8¼ × 11.   24801-1 Pa. $10.95

THE STORY OF KING ARTHUR AND HIS KNIGHTS, Howard Pyle. Enchanting version of King Arthur fable has delighted generations with imaginative narratives of exciting adventures and unforgettable illustrations by the author. 41 illustrations. xviii + 313pp. 6⅛ × 9¼.   21445-1 Pa. $6.95

THE GODS OF THE EGYPTIANS, E. A. Wallis Budge. Thorough coverage of numerous gods of ancient Egypt by foremost Egyptologist. Information on evolution of cults, rites and gods; the cult of Osiris; the Book of the Dead and its rites; the sacred animals and birds; Heaven and Hell; and more. 956pp. 6⅛ × 9¼.
       22055-9, 22056-7 Pa., Two-vol. set $21.90

A THEOLOGICO-POLITICAL TREATISE, Benedict Spinoza. Also contains unfinished Political Treatise. Great classic on religious liberty, theory of government on common consent. R. Elwes translation. Total of 421pp. 5⅜ × 8½.
       20249-6 Pa. $7.95

INCIDENTS OF TRAVEL IN CENTRAL AMERICA, CHIAPAS, AND YUCATAN, John L. Stephens. Almost single-handed discovery of Maya culture; exploration of ruined cities, monuments, temples; customs of Indians. 115 drawings. 892pp. 5⅜ × 8½.   22404-X, 22405-8 Pa., Two-vol. set $15.90

LOS CAPRICHOS, Francisco Goya. 80 plates of wild, grotesque monsters and caricatures. Prado manuscript included. 183pp. 6⅛ × 9⅜.   22384-1 Pa. $5.95

AUTOBIOGRAPHY: The Story of My Experiments with Truth, Mohandas K. Gandhi. Not hagiography, but Gandhi in his own words. Boyhood, legal studies, purification, the growth of the Satyagraha (nonviolent protest) movement. Critical, inspiring work of the man who freed India. 480pp. 5⅜ × 8½. (Available in U.S. only)
       24593-4 Pa. $6.95

ILLUSTRATED DICTIONARY OF HISTORIC ARCHITECTURE, edited by Cyril M. Harris. Extraordinary compendium of clear, concise definitions for over 5,000 important architectural terms complemented by over 2,000 line drawings. Covers full spectrum of architecture from ancient ruins to 20th-century Modernism. Preface. 592pp. 7½ × 9⅝. 24444-X Pa. $15.95

THE NIGHT BEFORE CHRISTMAS, Clement Moore. Full text, and woodcuts from original 1848 book. Also critical, historical material. 19 illustrations. 40pp. 4⅝ × 6. 22797-9 Pa. $2.50

THE LESSON OF JAPANESE ARCHITECTURE: 165 Photographs, Jiro Harada. Memorable gallery of 165 photographs taken in the 1930's of exquisite Japanese homes of the well-to-do and historic buildings. 13 line diagrams. 192pp. 8⅝ × 11¼. 24778-3 Pa. $10.95

THE AUTOBIOGRAPHY OF CHARLES DARWIN AND SELECTED LETTERS, edited by Francis Darwin. The fascinating life of eccentric genius composed of an intimate memoir by Darwin (intended for his children); commentary by his son, Francis; hundreds of fragments from notebooks, journals, papers; and letters to and from Lyell, Hooker, Huxley, Wallace and Henslow. xi + 365pp. 5⅜ × 8. 20479-0 Pa. $6.95

WONDERS OF THE SKY: Observing Rainbows, Comets, Eclipses, the Stars and Other Phenomena, Fred Schaaf. Charming, easy-to-read poetic guide to all manner of celestial events visible to the naked eye. Mock suns, glories, Belt of Venus, more. Illustrated. 299pp. 5¼ × 8¼. 24402-4 Pa. $7.95

BURNHAM'S CELESTIAL HANDBOOK, Robert Burnham, Jr. Thorough guide to the stars beyond our solar system. Exhaustive treatment. Alphabetical by constellation: Andromeda to Cetus in Vol. 1; Chamaeleon to Orion in Vol. 2; and Pavo to Vulpecula in Vol. 3. Hundreds of illustrations. Index in Vol. 3. 2,000pp. 6⅛ × 9¼. 23567-X, 23568-8, 23673-0 Pa., Three-vol. set $41.85

STAR NAMES: Their Lore and Meaning, Richard Hinckley Allen. Fascinating history of names various cultures have given to constellations and literary and folkloristic uses that have been made of stars. Indexes to subjects. Arabic and Greek names. Biblical references. Bibliography. 563pp. 5⅜ × 8½. 21079-0 Pa. $8.95

THIRTY YEARS THAT SHOOK PHYSICS: The Story of Quantum Theory, George Gamow. Lucid, accessible introduction to influential theory of energy and matter. Careful explanations of Dirac's anti-particles, Bohr's model of the atom, much more. 12 plates. Numerous drawings. 240pp. 5⅜ × 8½. 24895-X Pa. $5.95

CHINESE DOMESTIC FURNITURE IN PHOTOGRAPHS AND MEASURED DRAWINGS, Gustav Ecke. A rare volume, now affordably priced for antique collectors, furniture buffs and art historians. Detailed review of styles ranging from early Shang to late Ming. Unabridged republication. 161 black-and-white drawings, photos. Total of 224pp. 8⅜ × 11¼. (Available in U.S. only) 25171-3 Pa. $13.95

VINCENT VAN GOGH: A Biography, Julius Meier-Graefe. Dynamic, penetrating study of artist's life, relationship with brother, Theo, painting techniques, travels, more. Readable, engrossing. 160pp. 5⅜ × 8½. (Available in U.S. only) 25253-1 Pa. $4.95

HOW TO WRITE, Gertrude Stein. Gertrude Stein claimed anyone could understand her unconventional writing—here are clues to help. Fascinating improvisations, language experiments, explanations illuminate Stein's craft and the art of writing. Total of 414pp. 4⅜ × 6⅜. 23144-5 Pa. $6.95

ADVENTURES AT SEA IN THE GREAT AGE OF SAIL: Five Firsthand Narratives, edited by Elliot Snow. Rare true accounts of exploration, whaling, shipwreck, fierce natives, trade, shipboard life, more. 33 illustrations. Introduction. 353pp. 5⅜ × 8½. 25177-2 Pa. $8.95

THE HERBAL OR GENERAL HISTORY OF PLANTS, John Gerard. Classic descriptions of about 2,850 plants—with over 2,700 illustrations—includes Latin and English names, physical descriptions, varieties, time and place of growth, more. 2,706 illustrations. xlv + 1,678pp. 8½ × 12¼. 23147-X Cloth. $75.00

DOROTHY AND THE WIZARD IN OZ, L. Frank Baum. Dorothy and the Wizard visit the center of the Earth, where people are vegetables, glass houses grow and Oz characters reappear. Classic sequel to *Wizard of Oz*. 256pp. 5⅜ × 8. 24714-7 Pa. $5.95

SONGS OF EXPERIENCE: Facsimile Reproduction with 26 Plates in Full Color, William Blake. This facsimile of Blake's original "Illuminated Book" reproduces 26 full-color plates from a rare 1826 edition. Includes "The Tyger," "London," "Holy Thursday," and other immortal poems. 26 color plates. Printed text of poems. 48pp. 5¼ × 7. 24636-1 Pa. $3.95

SONGS OF INNOCENCE, William Blake. The first and most popular of Blake's famous "Illuminated Books," in a facsimile edition reproducing all 31 brightly colored plates. Additional printed text of each poem. 64pp. 5¼ × 7. 22764-2 Pa. $3.95

PRECIOUS STONES, Max Bauer. Classic, thorough study of diamonds, rubies, emeralds, garnets, etc.: physical character, occurrence, properties, use, similar topics. 20 plates, 8 in color. 94 figures. 659pp. 6⅛ × 9¼. 21910-0, 21911-9 Pa., Two-vol. set $15.90

ENCYCLOPEDIA OF VICTORIAN NEEDLEWORK, S. F. A. Caulfeild and Blanche Saward. Full, precise descriptions of stitches, techniques for dozens of needlecrafts—most exhaustive reference of its kind. Over 800 figures. Total of 679pp. 8⅛ × 11. Two volumes. Vol. 1 22800-2 Pa. $11.95
Vol. 2 22801-0 Pa. $11.95

THE MARVELOUS LAND OF OZ, L. Frank Baum. Second Oz book, the Scarecrow and Tin Woodman are back with hero named Tip, Oz magic. 136 illustrations. 287pp. 5⅜ × 8½. 20692-0 Pa. $5.95

WILD FOWL DECOYS, Joel Barber. Basic book on the subject, by foremost authority and collector. Reveals history of decoy making and rigging, place in American culture, different kinds of decoys, how to make them, and how to use them. 140 plates. 156pp. 7⅞ × 10¾. 20011-6 Pa. $8.95

HISTORY OF LACE, Mrs. Bury Palliser. Definitive, profusely illustrated chronicle of lace from earliest times to late 19th century. Laces of Italy, Greece, England, France, Belgium, etc. Landmark of needlework scholarship. 266 illustrations. 672pp. 6⅛ × 9¼. 24742-2 Pa. $14.95

ILLUSTRATED GUIDE TO SHAKER FURNITURE, Robert Meader. All furniture and appurtenances, with much on unknown local styles. 235 photos. 146pp. 9 × 12. 22819-3 Pa. $8.95

WHALE SHIPS AND WHALING: A Pictorial Survey, George Francis Dow. Over 200 vintage engravings, drawings, photographs of barks, brigs, cutters, other vessels. Also harpoons, lances, whaling guns, many other artifacts. Comprehensive text by foremost authority. 207 black-and-white illustrations. 288pp. 6 × 9. 24808-9 Pa. $9.95

THE BERTRAMS, Anthony Trollope. Powerful portrayal of blind self-will and thwarted ambition includes one of Trollope's most heartrending love stories. 497pp. 5⅜ × 8½. 25119-5 Pa. $9.95

ADVENTURES WITH A HAND LENS, Richard Headstrom. Clearly written guide to observing and studying flowers and grasses, fish scales, moth and insect wings, egg cases, buds, feathers, seeds, leaf scars, moss, molds, ferns, common crystals, etc.—all with an ordinary, inexpensive magnifying glass. 209 exact line drawings aid in your discoveries. 220pp. 5⅜ × 8½. 23330-8 Pa. $4.95

RODIN ON ART AND ARTISTS, Auguste Rodin. Great sculptor's candid, wide-ranging comments on meaning of art; great artists; relation of sculpture to poetry, painting, music; philosophy of life, more. 76 superb black-and-white illustrations of Rodin's sculpture, drawings and prints. 119pp. 8⅜ × 11¼. 24487-3 Pa. $7.95

FIFTY CLASSIC FRENCH FILMS, 1912–1982: A Pictorial Record, Anthony Slide. Memorable stills from Grand Illusion, Beauty and the Beast, Hiroshima, Mon Amour, many more. Credits, plot synopses, reviews, etc. 160pp. 8¼ × 11. 25256-6 Pa. $11.95

THE PRINCIPLES OF PSYCHOLOGY, William James. Famous long course complete, unabridged. Stream of thought, time perception, memory, experimental methods; great work decades ahead of its time. 94 figures. 1,391pp. 5⅜ × 8½. 20381-6, 20382-4 Pa., Two-vol. set $23.90

BODIES IN A BOOKSHOP, R. T. Campbell. Challenging mystery of blackmail and murder with ingenious plot and superbly drawn characters. In the best tradition of British suspense fiction. 192pp. 5⅜ × 8½. 24720-1 Pa. $4.95

CALLAS: PORTRAIT OF A PRIMA DONNA, George Jellinek. Renowned commentator on the musical scene chronicles incredible career and life of the most controversial, fascinating, influential operatic personality of our time. 64 black-and-white photographs. 416pp. 5⅜ × 8¼. 25047-4 Pa. $8.95

GEOMETRY, RELATIVITY AND THE FOURTH DIMENSION, Rudolph Rucker. Exposition of fourth dimension, concepts of relativity as Flatland characters continue adventures. Popular, easily followed yet accurate, profound. 141 illustrations. 133pp. 5⅜ × 8½. 23400-2 Pa. $4.95

HOUSEHOLD STORIES BY THE BROTHERS GRIMM, with pictures by Walter Crane. 53 classic stories—Rumpelstiltskin, Rapunzel, Hansel and Gretel, the Fisherman and his Wife, Snow White, Tom Thumb, Sleeping Beauty, Cinderella, and so much more—lavishly illustrated with original 19th century drawings. 114 illustrations. x + 269pp. 5⅜ × 8½. 21080-4 Pa. $4.95

SUNDIALS, Albert Waugh. Far and away the best, most thorough coverage of ideas, mathematics concerned, types, construction, adjusting anywhere. Over 100 illustrations. 230pp. 5⅜ × 8½. 22947-5 Pa. $5.95

PICTURE HISTORY OF THE NORMANDIE: With 190 Illustrations, Frank O. Braynard. Full story of legendary French ocean liner: Art Deco interiors, design innovations, furnishings, celebrities, maiden voyage, tragic fire, much more. Extensive text. 144pp. 8⅞ × 11¾. 25257-4 Pa. $10.95

THE FIRST AMERICAN COOKBOOK: A Facsimile of "American Cookery," 1796, Amelia Simmons. Facsimile of the first American-written cookbook published in the United States contains authentic recipes for colonial favorites—pumpkin pudding, winter squash pudding, spruce beer, Indian slapjacks, and more. Introductory Essay and Glossary of colonial cooking terms. 80pp. 5⅜ × 8½. 24710-4 Pa. $3.50

101 PUZZLES IN THOUGHT AND LOGIC, C. R. Wylie, Jr. Solve murders and robberies, find out which fishermen are liars, how a blind man could possibly identify a color—purely by your own reasoning! 107pp. 5⅜ × 8½. 20367-0 Pa. $2.50

ANCIENT EGYPTIAN MYTHS AND LEGENDS, Lewis Spence. Examines animism, totemism, fetishism, creation myths, deities, alchemy, art and magic, other topics. Over 50 illustrations. 432pp. 5⅜ × 8½. 26525-0 Pa. $8.95

ANTHROPOLOGY AND MODERN LIFE, Franz Boas. Great anthropologist's classic treatise on race and culture. Introduction by Ruth Bunzel. Only inexpensive paperback edition. 255pp. 5⅜ × 8½. 25245-0 Pa. $6.95

THE TALE OF PETER RABBIT, Beatrix Potter. The inimitable Peter's terrifying adventure in Mr. McGregor's garden, with all 27 wonderful, full-color Potter illustrations. 55pp. 4¼ × 5½. (Available in U.S. only) 22827-4 Pa. $1.75

THREE PROPHETIC SCIENCE FICTION NOVELS, H. G. Wells. *When the Sleeper Wakes, A Story of the Days to Come* and *The Time Machine* (full version). 335pp. 5⅜ × 8½. (Available in U.S. only) 20605-X Pa. $6.95

APICIUS COOKERY AND DINING IN IMPERIAL ROME, edited and translated by Joseph Dommers Vehling. Oldest known cookbook in existence offers readers a clear picture of what foods Romans ate, how they prepared them, etc. 49 illustrations. 301pp. 6⅛ × 9¼. 23563-7 Pa. $7.95

SHAKESPEARE LEXICON AND QUOTATION DICTIONARY, Alexander Schmidt. Full definitions, locations, shades of meaning of every word in plays and poems. More than 50,000 exact quotations. 1,485pp. 6½ × 9¼. 22726-X, 22727-8 Pa., Two-vol. set $31.90

THE WORLD'S GREAT SPEECHES, edited by Lewis Copeland and Lawrence W. Lamm. Vast collection of 278 speeches from Greeks to 1970. Powerful and effective models; unique look at history. 842pp. 5⅜ × 8½. 20468-5 Pa. $12.95

THE BLUE FAIRY BOOK, Andrew Lang. The first, most famous collection, with many familiar tales: Little Red Riding Hood, Aladdin and the Wonderful Lamp, Puss in Boots, Sleeping Beauty, Hansel and Gretel, Rumpelstiltskin; 37 in all. 138 illustrations. 390pp. 5⅜ × 8½. 21437-0 Pa. $6.95

THE STORY OF THE CHAMPIONS OF THE ROUND TABLE, Howard Pyle. Sir Launcelot, Sir Tristram and Sir Percival in spirited adventures of love and triumph retold in Pyle's inimitable style. 50 drawings, 31 full-page. xviii + 329pp. 6½ × 9¼. 21883-X Pa. $7.95

THE MYTHS OF THE NORTH AMERICAN INDIANS, Lewis Spence. Myths and legends of the Algonquins, Iroquois, Pawnees and Sioux with comprehensive historical and ethnological commentary. 36 illustrations. 5⅜ × 8½.
25967-6 Pa. $8.95

GREAT DINOSAUR HUNTERS AND THEIR DISCOVERIES, Edwin H. Colbert. Fascinating, lavishly illustrated chronicle of dinosaur research, 1820's to 1960. Achievements of Cope, Marsh, Brown, Buckland, Mantell, Huxley, many others. 384pp. 5¼ × 8¼. 24701-5 Pa. $7.95

THE TASTEMAKERS, Russell Lynes. Informal, illustrated social history of American taste 1850's-1950's. First popularized categories Highbrow, Lowbrow, Middlebrow. 129 illustrations. New (1979) afterword. 384pp. 6 × 9.
23993-4 Pa. $8.95

DOUBLE CROSS PURPOSES, Ronald A. Knox. A treasure hunt in the Scottish Highlands, an old map, unidentified corpse, surprise discoveries keep reader guessing in this cleverly intricate tale of financial skullduggery. 2 black-and-white maps. 320pp. 5⅜ × 8½. (Available in U.S. only) 25032-6 Pa. $6.95

AUTHENTIC VICTORIAN DECORATION AND ORNAMENTATION IN FULL COLOR: 46 Plates from "Studies in Design," Christopher Dresser. Superb full-color lithographs reproduced from rare original portfolio of a major Victorian designer. 48pp. 9¼ × 12¼. 25083-0 Pa. $7.95

PRIMITIVE ART, Franz Boas. Remains the best text ever prepared on subject, thoroughly discussing Indian, African, Asian, Australian, and, especially, Northern American primitive art. Over 950 illustrations show ceramics, masks, totem poles, weapons, textiles, paintings, much more. 376pp. 5⅜ × 8. 20025-6 Pa. $7.95

SIDELIGHTS ON RELATIVITY, Albert Einstein. Unabridged republication of two lectures delivered by the great physicist in 1920-21. *Ether and Relativity* and *Geometry and Experience*. Elegant ideas in non-mathematical form, accessible to intelligent layman. vi + 56pp. 5⅜ × 8½. 24511-X Pa. $2.95

THE WIT AND HUMOR OF OSCAR WILDE, edited by Alvin Redman. More than 1,000 ripostes, paradoxes, wisecracks: Work is the curse of the drinking classes, I can resist everything except temptation, etc. 258pp. 5⅜ × 8½. 20602-5 Pa. $4.95

ADVENTURES WITH A MICROSCOPE, Richard Headstrom. 59 adventures with clothing fibers, protozoa, ferns and lichens, roots and leaves, much more. 142 illustrations. 232pp. 5⅜ × 8½. 23471-1 Pa. $3.95

PLANTS OF THE BIBLE, Harold N. Moldenke and Alma L. Moldenke. Standard reference to all 230 plants mentioned in Scriptures. Latin name, biblical reference, uses, modern identity, much more. Unsurpassed encyclopedic resource for scholars, botanists, nature lovers, students of Bible. Bibliography. Indexes. 123 black-and-white illustrations. 384pp. 6 × 9. 25069-5 Pa. $8.95

FAMOUS AMERICAN WOMEN: A Biographical Dictionary from Colonial Times to the Present, Robert McHenry, ed. From Pocahontas to Rosa Parks, 1,035 distinguished American women documented in separate biographical entries. Accurate, up-to-date data, numerous categories, spans 400 years. Indices. 493pp. 6½ × 9¼. 24523-3 Pa. $10.95

THE FABULOUS INTERIORS OF THE GREAT OCEAN LINERS IN HISTORIC PHOTOGRAPHS, William H. Miller, Jr. Some 200 superb photographs capture exquisite interiors of world's great "floating palaces"—1890's to 1980's: *Titanic, Ile de France, Queen Elizabeth, United States, Europa,* more. Approx. 200 black-and-white photographs. Captions. Text. Introduction. 160pp. 8⅞ × 11¾. 24756-2 Pa. $9.95

THE GREAT LUXURY LINERS, 1927–1954: A Photographic Record, William H. Miller, Jr. Nostalgic tribute to heyday of ocean liners. 186 photos of Ile de France, Normandie, Leviathan, Queen Elizabeth, United States, many others. Interior and exterior views. Introduction. Captions. 160pp. 9 × 12. 24056-8 Pa. $10.95

A NATURAL HISTORY OF THE DUCKS, John Charles Phillips. Great landmark of ornithology offers complete detailed coverage of nearly 200 species and subspecies of ducks: gadwall, sheldrake, merganser, pintail, many more. 74 full-color plates, 102 black-and-white. Bibliography. Total of 1,920pp. 8⅝ × 11¼. 25141-1, 25142-X Cloth. Two-vol. set $100.00

THE SEAWEED HANDBOOK: An Illustrated Guide to Seaweeds from North Carolina to Canada, Thomas F. Lee. Concise reference covers 78 species. Scientific and common names, habitat, distribution, more. Finding keys for easy identification. 224pp. 5⅜ × 8½. 25215-9 Pa. $6.95

THE TEN BOOKS OF ARCHITECTURE: The 1755 Leoni Edition, Leon Battista Alberti. Rare classic helped introduce the glories of ancient architecture to the Renaissance. 68 black-and-white plates. 336pp. 8⅜ × 11¼. 25239-6 Pa. $14.95

MISS MACKENZIE, Anthony Trollope. Minor masterpieces by Victorian master unmasks many truths about life in 19th-century England. First inexpensive edition in years. 392pp. 5⅜ × 8½. 25201-9 Pa. $8.95

THE RIME OF THE ANCIENT MARINER, Gustave Doré, Samuel Taylor Coleridge. Dramatic engravings considered by many to be his greatest work. The terrifying space of the open sea, the storms and whirlpools of an unknown ocean, the ice of Antarctica, more—all rendered in a powerful, chilling manner. Full text. 38 plates. 77pp. 9¼ × 12. 22305-1 Pa. $4.95

THE EXPEDITIONS OF ZEBULON MONTGOMERY PIKE, Zebulon Montgomery Pike. Fascinating first-hand accounts (1805–6) of exploration of Mississippi River, Indian wars, capture by Spanish dragoons, much more. 1,088pp. 5⅜ × 8½. 25254-X, 25255-8 Pa. Two-vol. set $25.90

A CONCISE HISTORY OF PHOTOGRAPHY: Third Revised Edition, Helmut Gernsheim. Best one-volume history—camera obscura, photochemistry, daguerreotypes, evolution of cameras, film, more. Also artistic aspects—landscape, portraits, fine art, etc. 281 black-and-white photographs. 26 in color. 176pp. 8⅜ × 11¼. 25128-4 Pa. $13.95

THE DORÉ BIBLE ILLUSTRATIONS, Gustave Doré. 241 detailed plates from the Bible: the Creation scenes, Adam and Eve, Flood, Babylon, battle sequences, life of Jesus, etc. Each plate is accompanied by the verses from the King James version of the Bible. 241pp. 9 × 12. 23004-X Pa. $9.95

WANDERINGS IN WEST AFRICA, Richard F. Burton. Great Victorian scholar/adventurer's invaluable descriptions of African tribal rituals, fetishism, culture, art, much more. Fascinating 19th-century account. 624pp. 5⅜ × 8½. 26890-X Pa. $12.95

FLATLAND, E. A. Abbott. Intriguing and enormously popular science-fiction classic explores the complexities of trying to survive as a two-dimensional being in a three-dimensional world. Amusingly illustrated by the author. 16 illustrations. 103pp. 5⅜ × 8½. 20001-9 Pa. $2.50

THE HISTORY OF THE LEWIS AND CLARK EXPEDITION, Meriwether Lewis and William Clark, edited by Elliott Coues. Classic edition of Lewis and Clark's day-by-day journals that later became the basis for U.S. claims to Oregon and the West. Accurate and invaluable geographical, botanical, biological, meteorological and anthropological material. Total of 1,508pp. 5⅜ × 8½.
21268-8, 21269-6, 21270-X Pa. Three-vol. set $26.85

LANGUAGE, TRUTH AND LOGIC, Alfred J. Ayer. Famous, clear introduction to Vienna, Cambridge schools of Logical Positivism. Role of philosophy, elimination of metaphysics, nature of analysis, etc. 160pp. 5⅜ × 8½. (Available in U.S. and Canada only) 20010-8 Pa. $3.95

MATHEMATICS FOR THE NONMATHEMATICIAN, Morris Kline. Detailed, college-level treatment of mathematics in cultural and historical context, with numerous exercises. For liberal arts students. Preface. Recommended Reading Lists. Tables. Index. Numerous black-and-white figures. xvi + 641pp. 5⅜ × 8½.
24823-2 Pa. $11.95

HANDBOOK OF PICTORIAL SYMBOLS, Rudolph Modley. 3,250 signs and symbols, many systems in full; official or heavy commercial use. Arranged by subject. Most in Pictorial Archive series. 143pp. 8⅛ × 11. 23357-X Pa. $6.95

INCIDENTS OF TRAVEL IN YUCATAN, John L. Stephens. Classic (1843) exploration of jungles of Yucatan, looking for evidences of Maya civilization. Travel adventures, Mexican and Indian culture, etc. Total of 669pp. 5⅜ × 8½.
20926-1, 20927-X Pa., Two-vol. set $11.90

DEGAS: An Intimate Portrait, Ambroise Vollard. Charming, anecdotal memoir by famous art dealer of one of the greatest 19th-century French painters. 14 black-and-white illustrations. Introduction by Harold L. Van Doren. 96pp. 5⅜ × 8½.
25131-4 Pa. $4.95

PERSONAL NARRATIVE OF A PILGRIMAGE TO ALMANDINAH AND MECCAH, Richard Burton. Great travel classic by remarkably colorful personality. Burton, disguised as a Moroccan, visited sacred shrines of Islam, narrowly escaping death. 47 illustrations. 959pp. 5⅜ × 8½.   21217-3, 21218-1 Pa., Two-vol. set $19.90

PHRASE AND WORD ORIGINS, A. H. Holt. Entertaining, reliable, modern study of more than 1,200 colorful words, phrases, origins and histories. Much unexpected information. 254pp. 5⅜ × 8½.   20758-7 Pa. $5.95

THE RED THUMB MARK, R. Austin Freeman. In this first Dr. Thorndyke case, the great scientific detective draws fascinating conclusions from the nature of a single fingerprint. Exciting story, authentic science. 320pp. 5⅜ × 8½. (Available in U.S. only)   25210-8 Pa. $6.95

AN EGYPTIAN HIEROGLYPHIC DICTIONARY, E. A. Wallis Budge. Monumental work containing about 25,000 words or terms that occur in texts ranging from 3000 B.C. to 600 A.D. Each entry consists of a transliteration of the word, the word in hieroglyphs, and the meaning in English. 1,314pp. 6⅜ × 10.
23615-3, 23616-1 Pa., Two-vol. set $35.90

THE COMPLEAT STRATEGYST: Being a Primer on the Theory of Games of Strategy, J. D. Williams. Highly entertaining classic describes, with many illustrated examples, how to select best strategies in conflict situations. Prefaces. Appendices. xvi + 268pp. 5⅜ × 8½.   25101-2 Pa. $6.95

THE ROAD TO OZ, L. Frank Baum. Dorothy meets the Shaggy Man, little Button-Bright and the Rainbow's beautiful daughter in this delightful trip to the magical Land of Oz. 272pp. 5⅜ × 8.   25208-6 Pa. $5.95

POINT AND LINE TO PLANE, Wassily Kandinsky. Seminal exposition of role of point, line, other elements in non-objective painting. Essential to understanding 20th-century art. 127 Illustrations. 192pp. 6½ × 9¼.   23808-3 Pa. $5.95

LADY ANNA, Anthony Trollope. Moving chronicle of Countess Lovel's bitter struggle to win for herself and daughter Anna their rightful rank and fortune—perhaps at cost of sanity itself. 384pp. 5⅜ × 8½.   24669-8 Pa. $8.95

EGYPTIAN MAGIC, E. A. Wallis Budge. Sums up all that is known about magic in Ancient Egypt: the role of magic in controlling the gods, powerful amulets that warded off evil spirits, scarabs of immortality, use of wax images, formulas and spells, the secret name, much more. 253pp. 5⅜ × 8½.   22681-6 Pa. $4.50

THE DANCE OF SIVA, Ananda Coomaraswamy. Preeminent authority unfolds the vast metaphysic of India: the revelation of her art, conception of the universe, social organization, etc. 27 reproductions of art masterpieces. 192pp. 5⅜ × 8½.
24817-8 Pa. $5.95

CHRISTMAS CUSTOMS AND TRADITIONS, Clement A. Miles. Origin, evolution, significance of religious, secular practices. Caroling, gifts, yule logs, much more. Full, scholarly yet fascinating; non-sectarian. 400pp. 5⅜ × 8½.

23354-5 Pa. $6.95

THE HUMAN FIGURE IN MOTION, Eadweard Muybridge. More than 4,500 stopped-action photos, in action series, showing undraped men, women, children jumping, lying down, throwing, sitting, wrestling, carrying, etc. 390pp. 7⅞ × 10⅝.

20204-6 Cloth. $24.95

THE MAN WHO WAS THURSDAY, Gilbert Keith Chesterton. Witty, fast-paced novel about a club of anarchists in turn-of-the-century London. Brilliant social, religious, philosophical speculations. 128pp. 5⅜ × 8½.

25121-7 Pa. $3.95

A CEZANNE SKETCHBOOK: Figures, Portraits, Landscapes and Still Lifes, Paul Cezanne. Great artist experiments with tonal effects, light, mass, other qualities in over 100 drawings. A revealing view of developing master painter, precursor of Cubism. 102 black-and-white illustrations. 144pp. 8¾ × 6⅝.

24790-2 Pa. $6.95

AN ENCYCLOPEDIA OF BATTLES: Accounts of Over 1,560 Battles from 1479 B.C. to the Present, David Eggenberger. Presents essential details of every major battle in recorded history, from the first battle of Megiddo in 1479 B.C. to Grenada in 1984. List of Battle Maps. New Appendix covering the years 1967–1984. Index. 99 illustrations. 544pp. 6½ × 9¼.

24913-1 Pa. $14.95

AN ETYMOLOGICAL DICTIONARY OF MODERN ENGLISH, Ernest Weekley. Richest, fullest work, by foremost British lexicographer. Detailed word histories. Inexhaustible. Total of 856pp. 6½ × 9¼.

21873-2, 21874-0 Pa., Two-vol. set $19.90

WEBSTER'S AMERICAN MILITARY BIOGRAPHIES, edited by Robert McHenry. Over 1,000 figures who shaped 3 centuries of American military history. Detailed biographies of Nathan Hale, Douglas MacArthur, Mary Hallaren, others. Chronologies of engagements, more. Introduction. Addenda. 1,033 entries in alphabetical order. xi + 548pp. 6½ × 9¼. (Available in U.S. only)

24758-9 Pa. $13.95

LIFE IN ANCIENT EGYPT, Adolf Erman. Detailed older account, with much not in more recent books: domestic life, religion, magic, medicine, commerce, and whatever else needed for complete picture. Many illustrations. 597pp. 5⅜ × 8½.

22632-8 Pa. $8.95

HISTORIC COSTUME IN PICTURES, Braun & Schneider. Over 1,450 costumed figures shown, covering a wide variety of peoples: kings, emperors, nobles, priests, servants, soldiers, scholars, townsfolk, peasants, merchants, courtiers, cavaliers, and more. 256pp. 8⅜ × 11¼.

23150-X Pa. $9.95

THE NOTEBOOKS OF LEONARDO DA VINCI, edited by J. P. Richter. Extracts from manuscripts reveal great genius; on painting, sculpture, anatomy, sciences, geography, etc. Both Italian and English. 186 ms. pages reproduced, plus 500 additional drawings, including studies for *Last Supper, Sforza* monument, etc. 860pp. 7⅞ × 10¾. (Available in U.S. only) 22572-0, 22573-9 Pa., Two-vol. set $31.90

THE ART NOUVEAU STYLE BOOK OF ALPHONSE MUCHA: All 72 Plates from "Documents Decoratifs" in Original Color, Alphonse Mucha. Rare copyright-free design portfolio by high priest of Art Nouveau. Jewelry, wallpaper, stained glass, furniture, figure studies, plant and animal motifs, etc. Only complete one-volume edition. 80pp. 9⅜ × 12¼. 24044-4 Pa. $9.95

ANIMALS: 1,419 COPYRIGHT-FREE ILLUSTRATIONS OF MAMMALS, BIRDS, FISH, INSECTS, ETC., edited by Jim Harter. Clear wood engravings present, in extremely lifelike poses, over 1,000 species of animals. One of the most extensive pictorial sourcebooks of its kind. Captions. Index. 284pp. 9 × 12. 23766-4 Pa. $9.95

OBELISTS FLY HIGH, C. Daly King. Masterpiece of American detective fiction, long out of print, involves murder on a 1935 transcontinental flight—"a very thrilling story"—NY Times. Unabridged and unaltered republication of the edition published by William Collins Sons & Co. Ltd., London, 1935. 288pp. 5⅜ × 8½. (Available in U.S. only) 25036-9 Pa. $5.95

VICTORIAN AND EDWARDIAN FASHION: A Photographic Survey, Alison Gernsheim. First fashion history completely illustrated by contemporary photographs. Full text plus 235 photos, 1840–1914, in which many celebrities appear. 240pp. 6½ × 9¼. 24205-6 Pa. $8.95

THE ART OF THE FRENCH ILLUSTRATED BOOK, 1700–1914, Gordon N. Ray. Over 630 superb book illustrations by Fragonard, Delacroix, Daumier, Doré, Grandville, Manet, Mucha, Steinlen, Toulouse-Lautrec and many others. Preface. Introduction. 633 halftones. Indices of artists, authors & titles, binders and provenances. Appendices. Bibliography. 608pp. 8⅜ × 11¼. 25086-5 Pa. $24.95

THE WONDERFUL WIZARD OF OZ, L. Frank Baum. Facsimile in full color of America's finest children's classic. 143 illustrations by W. W. Denslow. 267pp. 5⅜ × 8½. 20691-2 Pa. $7.95

FOLLOWING THE EQUATOR: A Journey Around the World, Mark Twain. Great writer's 1897 account of circumnavigating the globe by steamship. Ironic humor, keen observations, vivid and fascinating descriptions of exotic places. 197 illustrations. 720pp. 5⅜ × 8½. 26113-1 Pa. $15.95

THE FRIENDLY STARS, Martha Evans Martin & Donald Howard Menzel. Classic text marshalls the stars together in an engaging, non-technical survey, presenting them as sources of beauty in night sky. 23 illustrations. Foreword. 2 star charts. Index. 147pp. 5⅜ × 8½. 21099-5 Pa. $3.95

FADS AND FALLACIES IN THE NAME OF SCIENCE, Martin Gardner. Fair, witty appraisal of cranks, quacks, and quackeries of science and pseudoscience: hollow earth, Velikovsky, orgone energy, Dianetics, flying saucers, Bridey Murphy, food and medical fads, etc. Revised, expanded In the Name of Science. "A very able and even-tempered presentation."—The New Yorker. 363pp. 5⅜ × 8. 20394-8 Pa. $6.95

ANCIENT EGYPT: ITS CULTURE AND HISTORY, J. E Manchip White. From pre-dynastics through Ptolemies: society, history, political structure, religion, daily life, literature, cultural heritage. 48 plates. 217pp. 5⅜ × 8½. 22548-8 Pa. $5.95

CATALOG OF DOVER BOOKS

SIR HARRY HOTSPUR OF HUMBLETHWAITE, Anthony Trollope. Incisive, unconventional psychological study of a conflict between a wealthy baronet, his idealistic daughter, and their scapegrace cousin. The 1870 novel in its first inexpensive edition in years. 250pp. 5⅜ × 8½.　　　　24953-0 Pa. $6.95

LASERS AND HOLOGRAPHY, Winston E. Kock. Sound introduction to burgeoning field, expanded (1981) for second edition. Wave patterns, coherence, lasers, diffraction, zone plates, properties of holograms, recent advances. 84 illustrations. 160pp. 5⅜ × 8¼. (Except in United Kingdom)　　24041-X Pa. $3.95

INTRODUCTION TO ARTIFICIAL INTELLIGENCE: SECOND, EN-LARGED EDITION, Philip C. Jackson, Jr. Comprehensive survey of artificial intelligence—the study of how machines (computers) can be made to act intelligently. Includes introductory and advanced material. Extensive notes updating the main text. 132 black-and-white illustrations. 512pp. 5⅜ × 8½.　　24864-X Pa. $8.95

HISTORY OF INDIAN AND INDONESIAN ART, Ananda K. Coomaraswamy. Over 400 illustrations illuminate classic study of Indian art from earliest Harappa finds to early 20th century. Provides philosophical, religious and social insights. 304pp. 6⅜ × 9⅜.　　　　25005-9 Pa. $11.95

THE GOLEM, Gustav Meyrink. Most famous supernatural novel in modern European literature, set in Ghetto of Old Prague around 1890. Compelling story of mystical experiences, strange transformations, profound terror. 13 black-and-white illustrations. 224pp. 5⅜ × 8½. (Available in U.S. only)　　25025-3 Pa. $6.95

PICTORIAL ENCYCLOPEDIA OF HISTORIC ARCHITECTURAL PLANS, DETAILS AND ELEMENTS: With 1,880 Line Drawings of Arches, Domes, Doorways, Facades, Gables, Windows, etc., John Theodore Haneman. Sourcebook of inspiration for architects, designers, others. Bibliography. Captions. 141pp. 9 × 12.　　　　24605-1 Pa. $7.95

BENCHLEY LOST AND FOUND, Robert Benchley. Finest humor from early 30's, about pet peeves, child psychologists, post office and others. Mostly unavailable elsewhere. 73 illustrations by Peter Arno and others. 183pp. 5⅜ × 8½.
　　　　22410-4 Pa. $4.95

ERTÉ GRAPHICS, Erté. Collection of striking color graphics: *Seasons, Alphabet, Numerals, Aces* and *Precious Stones*. 50 plates, including 4 on covers. 48pp. 9⅜ × 12¼.　　　　23580-7 Pa. $7.95

THE JOURNAL OF HENRY D. THOREAU, edited by Bradford Torrey, F. H. Allen. Complete reprinting of 14 volumes, 1837–61, over two million words; the sourcebooks for *Walden*, etc. Definitive. All original sketches, plus 75 photographs. 1,804pp. 8½ × 12¼.　　20312-3, 20313-1 Cloth., Two-vol. set $125.00

CASTLES: THEIR CONSTRUCTION AND HISTORY, Sidney Toy. Traces castle development from ancient roots. Nearly 200 photographs and drawings illustrate moats, keeps, baileys, many other features. Caernarvon, Dover Castles, Hadrian's Wall, Tower of London, dozens more. 256pp. 5⅜ × 8¼.
　　　　24898-4 Pa. $6.95

AMERICAN CLIPPER SHIPS: 1833–1858, Octavius T. Howe & Frederick C. Matthews. Fully-illustrated, encyclopedic review of 352 clipper ships from the period of America's greatest maritime supremacy. Introduction. 109 halftones. 5 black-and-white line illustrations. Index. Total of 928pp. 5⅜ × 8½.
25115-2, 25116-0 Pa., Two-vol. set $17.90

TOWARDS A NEW ARCHITECTURE, Le Corbusier. Pioneering manifesto by great architect, near legendary founder of "International School." Technical and aesthetic theories, views on industry, economics, relation of form to function, "mass-production spirit," much more. Profusely illustrated. Unabridged translation of 13th French edition. Introduction by Frederick Etchells. 320pp. 6⅛ × 9¼. (Available in U.S. only)
25023-7 Pa. $8.95

THE BOOK OF KELLS, edited by Blanche Cirker. Inexpensive collection of 32 full-color, full-page plates from the greatest illuminated manuscript of the Middle Ages, painstakingly reproduced from rare facsimile edition. Publisher's Note. Captions. 32pp. 9⅜ × 12¼.
24345-1 Pa. $4.95

BEST SCIENCE FICTION STORIES OF H. G. WELLS, H. G. Wells. Full novel *The Invisible Man*, plus 17 short stories: "The Crystal Egg," "Aepyornis Island," "The Strange Orchid," etc. 303pp. 5⅜ × 8½. (Available in U.S. only)
21531-8 Pa. $6.95

AMERICAN SAILING SHIPS: Their Plans and History, Charles G. Davis. Photos, construction details of schooners, frigates, clippers, other sailcraft of 18th to early 20th centuries—plus entertaining discourse on design, rigging, nautical lore, much more. 137 black-and-white illustrations. 240pp. 6⅛ × 9¼.
24658-2 Pa. $6.95

ENTERTAINING MATHEMATICAL PUZZLES, Martin Gardner. Selection of author's favorite conundrums involving arithmetic, money, speed, etc., with lively commentary. Complete solutions. 112pp. 5⅜ × 8½.
25211-6 Pa. $2.95

THE WILL TO BELIEVE, HUMAN IMMORTALITY, William James. Two books bound together. Effect of irrational on logical, and arguments for human immortality. 402pp. 5⅜ × 8½.
20291-7 Pa. $7.95

THE HAUNTED MONASTERY and THE CHINESE MAZE MURDERS, Robert Van Gulik. 2 full novels by Van Gulik continue adventures of Judge Dee and his companions. An evil Taoist monastery, seemingly supernatural events; overgrown topiary maze that hides strange crimes. Set in 7th-century China. 27 illustrations. 328pp. 5⅜ × 8½.
23502-5 Pa. $6.95

CELEBRATED CASES OF JUDGE DEE (DEE GOONG AN), translated by Robert Van Gulik. Authentic 18th-century Chinese detective novel; Dee and associates solve three interlocked cases. Led to Van Gulik's own stories with same characters. Extensive introduction. 9 illustrations. 237pp. 5⅜ × 8½.
23337-5 Pa. $5.95

Prices subject to change without notice.

Available at your book dealer or write for free catalog to Dept. GI, Dover Publications, Inc., 31 East 2nd St., Mineola, N.Y. 11501. Dover publishes more than 175 books each year on science, elementary and advanced mathematics, biology, music, art, literary history, social sciences and other areas.